WHAT PEOPL
The Imperfect J
MESSY
INTENTIONALITY

This is the perfect book to help us accept our imperfections. Nancy Kay gently guides you through the things that can hinder your growth into the qualities and inner work that lead you to an intentional path of living a life full of meaning, passion and contribution. Messy Intentionality is filled with wonderful examples of people who have transformed their lives, along with very practical exercises and checklists that support you along your journey to a more *aware life*.

——Dr. Judi Neal
Chairman and CEO of Edgewalkers
International Author of Edgewalkers:
People and Organizations that Take Risks,
Build Bridges, and Break New Ground

Nancy Kay is an inspiring coach who provides the reader tools to expand their hope, humility and gratitude – and thereby create more authenticity. This passionate, uplifting book is helpful for people who want a richer, more meaningful life now!

——Dr Jeffrey E. Auerbach, MCC
Vice President of International Coach Federation
Founder and President, College of Executive Coaching
Author of Personal and Executive Coaching: The Complete

Guide for Mental Health Professionals
We all long for authentic living, but often find it elusive and challenged in daily living. Yet authentic living actually leads to optimal living. In this inspirational book, Nancy Kay offers personal stories, useful tips and recipes for living more fully in a way that is practical and doable.

——Dr. Patrick Williams, MCC
CEO, Institute for Life Coach Training
Author of Becoming a Professional Life Coach: Lessons from the Institute of Life Coach Training

In an age of superficial relationships with ourselves and others, Nancy Kay has invited her readers to engage in exercises and insights that will take them to a place of authenticity and fulfillment. I recommend her book to anyone who is seeking to establish greater meaning for living, and improve how they relate to themselves and others!

—Dr. James S. Vuocolo
Master Certified Coach

THE IMPERFECT JOURNEY TO SELF-AWARENESS

MESSY
INTENTIONALITY

*Jenna —
I am so glad you are my friend! To your journey!
Love you,
Nancy S. Kay
10-28-16*

NANCY S. KAY

The Imperfect Journey to Self-Awareness

MESSY
INTENTIONALITY

TATE PUBLISHING
AND ENTERPRISES, LLC

Messy Intentionality
Copyright © 2016 by Nancy S. Kay. All rights reserved.

No part of this publication may be reproduced, stored in a retrieval system or transmitted in any way by any means, electronic, mechanical, photocopy, recording or otherwise without the prior permission of the author except as provided by USA copyright law.

This book is designed to provide accurate and authoritative information with regard to the subject matter covered. This information is given with the understanding that neither the author nor Tate Publishing, LLC is engaged in rendering legal, professional advice. Since the details of your situation are fact dependent, you should additionally seek the services of a competent professional.

The opinions expressed by the author are not necessarily those of Tate Publishing, LLC.

Published by Tate Publishing & Enterprises, LLC
127 E. Trade Center Terrace | Mustang, Oklahoma 73064 USA
1.888.361.9473 | www.tatepublishing.com

Tate Publishing is committed to excellence in the publishing industry. The company reflects the philosophy established by the founders, based on Psalm 68:11,
"*The Lord gave the word and great was the company of those who published it.*"

Book design copyright © 2016 by Tate Publishing, LLC. All rights reserved.
Cover design by Joana Quilantang
Interior design by Stephanie Woloszyn

Published in the United States of America

ISBN: 978-1-68270-583-4
1. Self-Help / Personal Growth / Happiness
2. Family & Relationships / Dysfunctional Families
16.09.26

ACKNOWLEDGMENTS

To Mom and Dad.
Your guidance and love are ever present!

To my dear friends and family who have journeyed with me.

And to my clients who have allowed me to journey with them.
Thank you!

CONTENTS

INTRODUCTION

PART I – THE UNAWARE LIFE
- Chapter 1: Messy
- Chapter 2: Longing
- Chapter 3: Losses
- Chapter 4: Betrayal

PART II – THE FOUR PILLARS
- Chapter 5: Optimism
- Chapter 6: Humility
- Chapter 7: Forgiveness
- Chapter 8: Gratitude

PART III – THE *AWARE LIFE*
- Chapter 9: Intentionality
- Chapter 10: Fulfillment
- Chapter 11: Finding Me Again

SELF-AWARENESS EXERCISES
ABOUT THE AUTHOR
NOTES

INTRODUCTION

Humans long for meaning, worth, connection, and yes, even... fun. And the only way to get what we long for is choosing to live—every day—with intention, purpose, and grace. Simply put, we decide to be aware and awake. Sounds easy? Well... it's anything but easy—yet, very rewarding in so many ways.

The intentional lifestyle is deeply personal and ultimately unique to each human being. There isn't a surefire way to tell you how to do it. It's a journey that belongs only to you, and it begins with self-awareness. It is an organic inner work you choose to enter into or ignore. You either stay asleep or wake up to the yearning that is beckoning you to join. At times, it will get messy, and you will make mistakes—yet each wrong turn will enlighten your life and your purpose, if you stay aware and awake. Being human is a work in progress, so be gentle with yourself. The road to living with genuine intention is bumpy and will have many detours, but it's worth it—so worth it.

My buried longings gave rise to this book. It began with a restless desire and a feeling of emptiness in the desert of my midlife when I came face to face with life—my life—as a collection of muddled choices. My people-pleasing personality was no longer useful. I lacked energy, fulfillment, and joy. I realized I was sacrificing too much of me to have peace with others. I realized my behavior came down to my fear of disappointing those I loved. There are many avenues to losing yourself, but caretaking was my primary poison.

This cage of fear accumulated into a lifestyle that had become exhaustive and ineffective. I not only questioned my beliefs—shaped by society's spoken and unspoken rules—but I also questioned who I was. I didn't know myself. I was living out a role of being a dutiful wife, stepmother, daughter, therapist...and I was exhausted! Yikes! How did I end up here?

It all started with listening to lies. The lies I told myself, lies others said to me, and entrenched lies of society. Lies about who I was supposed to be and how life was meant to look. I had to have a change in my life, just as I had encouraged and guided hundreds, if not thousands, to do in my workshops and counseling sessions. Now—it was my time!

This restless desire and emptiness led me to question and explore. I could have ignored my longings and lived with my head buried in the sand. Such a decision, or rather the lack of making a decision, would require forfeiting the newness of life that only comes from journeying. I faced the reality that I had based much of my life, and the decisions for my life, on faulty thinking.

More accurately, I lived from the lens of others. I had allowed my opinions, lifestyle, beliefs, and decisions to be overly influenced by others. I was thinking in a way that other people and archetypal societal structures had taught me to think and be. I have no one to blame for this; this time in my life simply was a wake-up call to my "voice," my soul, which beckoned me to journey.

I have experienced living an intentional life, and I fully believe that even a messy one can bring more significance, fulfillment, and meaning to life. Intentionality takes discipline, but it's not a to-do list. It's a choice to stop and pay attention to what is already there waiting for you. It's beckoning you to become aware. It's always there—waiting, calling, urging you to pause long enough to find your truth and embrace your passion. With intentional self-awareness, you can create the life you desire by consciously setting in motion the intent to make it happen.

The longing for an enlarged life—a life embracing more possibilities, growth, and freedom is many times the catalyst to choose this intentional journey toward the *aware life*. To be aware is to live honestly, genuinely, and purposefully to satisfy every aspect of your life. In my personal research with clients, I have come to realize there are four aspects essential to living the *aware life*: optimism, humility, forgiveness, and gratitude. These four pillars are attitudes and characteristics embedded in those who live a happy, peace-filled and fulfilling life.

The *aware life* has seasons and moments when aspects of your life have to be intentionally set aside, waiting for the right time to invest in that specific arena of your life, whether that's your health, work, relationships, spirituality, or personal self-care. Balance in all areas of your life is imperative. It just takes time, effort, and a lot of grace as you aspire to live a fully balanced, self-aware life.

Life is messy, things come up, and choices have to be made—nothing is clear. My heartfelt hope is that you find this book assists you on your intentional journey toward a more balanced, purposeful, and fulfilled life.

So, are you ready to trust your inner knowledge? To let the faint whisper of your inner voice guide you and give you strength? Do you desire to live in a manner that is intentionally and completely on purpose? Then it's time for you to choose to journey with intention—to be aware and awake—no matter the risk. Let's take the first step together.

PART ONE

THE UNAWARE LIFE

CHAPTER 1

MESSY

Life is messy—yet, it can become an incredible, mystifying, and fulfilling mess. Losses, disappointment, brokenness—are all common threads that bridge humankind. We desire connection and often experience loneliness; we want to have a purpose, yet we feel lost; we crave fulfillment, yet we feel empty. Being human is being messy. It is never clean cut. The journey is difficult. It is in awareness and in awakening that we truly start to see what life is meant to be. It is a gift. Indeed, a gift that connects each and every one of us.

On the pathway of life, decisions are made and often later regretted. A relationship starts with zest, yet often ends in bitterness and hurt. Jobs are lost, and dear ones get sick or even worse die. Life can change in a moment. Unexpected and unwanted events instantly change life. We are going to fail and make mistakes 10, 100, 1,000 times, but it's in the getting back up and moving forward where we find success.

The key to the *aware life* rests in intentionality. It is the purposeful and deliberate decision to become self-aware. This decision allows a way of life or rhythm to be created, and in this rhythm our future opens up in a new and powerful manner. Consequently, this decision will lead us to experience more love and fulfillment and become a more *loving* person. It's in self-awareness that we see our self fully. Then we are able to see others more objectively.

The first act of love is seeing a person as they truly are, not the way we want them to be. Self-awareness frees us and love frees others.

The act of seeing is courageous. Choosing to stay blind is imprisonment by fear—fear of failure, rejection, being found out, loss, and the unknown. Messy often happens when we put up every diversion and defense we can; when we choose not to embrace our fears. Subconsciously, we fight for what is safe, what we know—or as I will discuss later in the book—we want to stay in what is familiar—our "memory foam."

The journey to the *aware life* begins with courage, not fear. The great philosophers and religious leaders—including Augustine, Buddha, John of the Cross, and Teresa of Ávila—all taught their students and contemporaries to grow in self-awareness—not to stay stagnant, but to take risks.

So, what are we to do? I have condensed the journey into a three-step process that results in living the *aware life*. First, is **Awareness**. We must first concede that we are human and that our life is at times, if not always, messy, uptight, indolent, and so imperfect. We choose to change and want more for our life. We know only though self-awareness can life purpose and fulfillment we found. Second, is **Understanding**. We understand why we do the things we do. We no long live on auto-pilot, but are awake, aware, and present. This stage sometimes deems we find a professional counselor or coach to help shine insight into our current patterns and choices that are unhealthy and at times, destructive. Third, is **Intentionality**. In this stage we gather the courage to gently and lovingly grow and live a fuller, kinder, and on-purpose life. Intentionally changing old patterns and habits by embracing the messy in our life allows us to make different choices – ones that align with our values and beliefs.

It is in this risk-taking when transformation happens. It will not be as magical or perfect as when the caterpillar mysteriously and magically transforms into a beautiful, perfect butterfly. The road to human transformation is full of bumps and potholes and detours. It is not as delightful or quick as the emergence of the butterfly. Intentional human change is a lifelong process, which includes the following characteristics.

CONCEDING

The integration of imperfection starts in the realization of our worth—being loved—and yet still imperfect. Humans have a hard time loving what is not perfect. In fact, when imperfection happens, then condemnation starts within each of us. Feeling shame, guilt, and "less than" brings us first to be critical of our self, and then we let our cynical nature spread to the judgment of others. This judging of others relieves, if for only a few moments, the self-condemnation we have within ourselves from broken attachments and self-destructive behaviors.

This condemning, shame-filled and negative way of living leave us feeling alone, guilty, and afraid. It's in the acknowledgment of worthiness—of being loved by others, God – or whatever source you connect with, and includes self-love—only then we can embrace and accept our messy humanness. It prevents narcissism and entitlement by establishing a healthy self-esteem, which allows true self-love and love of others to grow. Acknowledging we don't have it all together is vital to the *aware life*. It's with humility and self-awareness that we find a more honest and peaceful life.

CHOOSE

The choice to become more aware begins by waking up and acknowledging that we are ready to have a different life—a richer life. The choice is just that—a choice. It's not the mustering of a plan for change; it's much deeper. It's commitment to our soul, to our heart, to our life—to be deliberate in how we choose to live our life.

Once we make the choice to start the intentional journey, we can't just simply walk away. The call to something more, something better will haunt us. This decision is to be taken seriously and with much thoughtfulness. We will not be able to walk comfortably away after we have invested in our life and decided to listen to the cry of our soul. Once we have chosen to journey, it will not easily be quiet again! The only way to silence your soul again is to go figuratively back to sleep by numbing ourselves with addictions, dependent relationships, and busyness.

COURAGE

Courage is the attribute required to change, to live differently, and to be more present in our everyday life. Courage is faith in action. It is faith that our life can be more fulfilling and much more authentic. Life can surely test us—illness, losing a loved one, loss of a relationship, or healing from past abuse or addiction.

Courage is what it takes to put the action in the healing. The real test of courage is to choose to live fully in an enlarged life, not slumbering in a cocoon of indifference. Our first step in climbing toward action for change is self-awareness. Self-awareness has many avenues, yet the one thread consistent in all the avenues is intentionality!

BE PRESENT

Recently, I took some time off work to have a modified sabbatical. I felt burned out, and I needed a break. Have you ever felt that way? I took off for the place that rejuvenates me more than any other place I know—the Rocky Mountains. One day, I went for a long hike with my dog—Clay. My intent was to listen quietly to my inner self. To eliminate the noise and listen to what my soul desired. What I heard from my soft inner voice was just STOP! Just stop! I waited longer until I could fully grasp what I needed.

What I heard was more profound and simpler than I expected: "Life opens up in the present—not in the future, and not in the past."

> *Life opens up in the present—not in the future,*
> *and not in the past.*

My soul beckoned me to stop, be present—be aware—live in the here and now. I needed to see who I was, feel what I was feeling, and carve out the time to be fully present. I had to intentionally let go and let whatever needed to happen—happen. If that was to lose a relationship, take more time for myself, recognize my shortcomings, mend a hurt, be less selfish, or take a risk, then I had to do it. I had to respond and embrace my fear. The fear of disappointing those I care for and grapple with their possible disapproval. I also had to accept the fear of seeing myself differently. Letting my faulty ego die. My false-self begrudgingly moved over to make room for my true-self. Demanding courage and risk.

Our false-self is the characteristics and beliefs we function from when we feel insecure. The true-self is like a baby learning to walk—falling with every other step he takes. Continuing to get back up and walk again. It's courage that keeps us from being victim to our failures. Just like the toddler, we must be courageous and walk again.

If we desire perfection and put demands on ourself to be faultless, we will create a sure plan for a stressful and unhappy life.

Having the courage to accept yourself fully as less than perfect is the first step in change. Courage facilitates the desire to be present, to hear our inner voice, and to move forward. It's the ability to experience ourself and others in the moment. We see things as they are; not how we dreamed them to be. We're awake and alert to what is before us. We're more emotionally and spiritually awake than we ever thought we could be.

Wholehearted living focuses on being fully aware and in the present; we can appreciate life—our life—for whatever it is. We experience more positive emotions and have less guilt, shame, and regrets.

SELF-AWARENESS

As Anne Lamott says, "There is ecstasy in paying attention."[1] It is true that a little introspection, a little pondering, will go a long way. Paying attention to our life means being self-aware. And it also means telling the truth—both to ourselves and others. So, what is self-awareness? I believe it is the clear perception of our personality, values, needs, habits, and emotions. It also includes our understand of other people, how they perceive us, our attitude and our responses to them. Having self-awareness allows us to see where our thoughts and emotions are guiding us. It also enables knowing ourselves well enough to control our feelings and behaviors and enhance our life and our relationships.

Self-awareness is the first step in creating what we want and mastering our life. It involves our emotions, reactions, personality, and behavior. Emotional Intelligence is the innate potential to manage, understand and explain emotions. Research has proven that 83% of all successful people have high self-awareness.[2] It's the vital process for living the *aware life*. Dr. Steven J. Stein and Howard E. Book in their book – The EQ Edge state:

"Emotional self-awareness is the foundation on which most of the other elements of emotional intelligence are built, the necessary first step toward exploring and coming to understand yourself, and toward change. Obviously, what you don't recognize, you can't manage. If you aren't aware of what you're doing, why you're doing it, and the way it's affecting others, you can't change."[3]

What gets in the way of being self-aware? The answer lies in the subconscious. Self-awareness is digging up and exploring old roles, and life scripts lived out unknowingly. Lies and cognitive distortion of who we think we are and what we should be dangle in our subconscious. These cognitive distortions mixed with fear, anxiety, and anger manifests into a false-self. Developing self-awareness is essential to make changes in our thoughts and behaviors.

Changing the interpretation of an event in our mind allows us to change our emotion around the event. Relationships are significantly affected by self-awareness or rather the lack of self-awareness. I'm sure we all would agree that relationships, even romantic relationships can be smooth sailing until there is some type of emotional hurt or unmet expectation. Having a clear understanding of our thoughts and behaviors facilitates our ability to manage our emotions so we can have healthy responses and make wise decisions.

CORE AREAS OF SELF-AWARENESS

Knowing ourselves involves identifying the different aspects of who we are. Human beings are multifaceted. Self-awareness is understanding what drives us to do the things we do. It's tuning into our energy and being aware of how we feel, knowing our personality, our wounds, our values, our needs and our distractions. It takes time and a commitment to paying attention to these areas, but I can't stress how important it is to live a fulfilled life.

When we aren't sure of a decision or want to make sure we are living a life that is aligned authentically with who we are and our values I suggest you check your energy. Take a moment and check-in with how you feel. Is your energy positive and productive or do you feel sad, fatigued or sluggish? These are good indicators to establish if you are or aren't congruent with the following core areas of self-awareness.

1. **Values**: Your core, personal values are what drive your actions. Whether we are consciously aware of them or not, we have many personal values. And these values are consistent and guide most, if not all, of our decisions. Your values are the qualities which are most important to you.

   Values guiding your life may include: Achievement. Adventure. Cooperation. Family. Friends. Kindness. Helping Others. Spirituality... When you are aware of your values and living according to them, you are more likely to accomplish what you deem is most important. And this will bring more fulfillment and depth to your life.

2. **Emotional Needs**: These are the psychological needs that drive behavior. When not met, they produce stress and drain your energy. Researchers, such as Maslow, identified common behaviors driven by your emotional and psychological needs. The need for affection, self-esteem, belonging, purpose, self-actualization, and power and control all fall into this category. They are your common motivators behind the decisions and actions you take. Understanding your strongest

needs allows you to manage yourself and your relationships best.

For example, let's say you have a high need for belonging—you may find yourself avoiding conflict and never voicing your opinion, allowing you to stay in the familiar place of belonging. This need may produce happiness and satisfaction, however, if belonging is too important and the environment is toxic, the emotional need for belonging can lead to a lack of fulfillment, anxiety, and depression. Self-awareness is vital for understanding your emotional needs and managing these needs in a healthy way.

3. **Lifestyle**: Your lifestyle is the manner you live routinely and often automatically. They are habits you do daily. You want to live a certain style, so you customize your life to live that way. By choosing work, activities, and relationships that honor your values, you find you are living the *aware life*. But, sometimes we choose habits that decrease our fulfillment and relationships effectiveness. For example, if you routinely make important decisions without consulting your spouse – he may not be compliant with those decisions. He may not just "go along" with what you decide or even worse it may build a quiet resentment inside him that will spill out in a wrath one day.

4. **Emotional Awareness**: To have an understanding of your feelings, what causes them, and how they impact your thoughts and actions is emotional awareness. At times we experience triggers that engage specific emotions, and we have a reaction that does not fit the situation. Understanding your emotions is powerful at these times. Emotional awareness helps you calm yourself when you need to; figure out why spending time with a particular friend is draining

your energy, or why the comment from your boss triggered such a strong response. The more emotional awareness you have, the greater control and management of your emotions you will have.

The truth is that almost any moment offers you an opportunity to live out your purpose and reinvent your soul. Spending a little time on self-discovery will uncover answers to mysteries you may have never known existed yet where in control of how you live your daily life.

Real living, or rather living a real and genuine life, starts with intentional self-awareness. The journey to the *aware life* is not a license for insensitivity or rudeness to others. As Anne Lamott, famed writer and political activist, says to be self-aware, we must not turn our eyes inward only—reading our autobiography and performing a one-person play. Being self-aware does not give license to inconsideration of others.[4] It's also not hedonistic, based on a raw subjective feelings that maximizes pleasure and minimizes pain no matter what the consequences are to others. Rather, self-awareness is in being genuine in our relationships. Kindness and grace is required at all times. Self-awareness is neither emotional vomiting nor sharing our life story with everyone. It's not about telling every person in our life all our struggles or fears, but it is about choosing a few trusted people with whom we can share those intimate insights and inviting them to join you in this sacred journey of self-discovery.

DISCOVERING YOUR VALUES

The truth is that almost any moment offers us an opportunity to live out our purpose and reinvent our soul. By choosing work, activities, and relationships that honor our values, we find we are living the *aware life*. Values release tremendous potential for success and happiness. Living life in line with what we value is important for a sense of well-being, while on the other hand, living a life that violates our values leads to frustration and depression. Our values are the deepest, most powerful forces in our lives.

There are two levels of values. First, there are the superficial shoulds. These are the relatively shallow values, which we are all expected to follow. They are primarily subconscious. (A few examples are waiting in line patiently or paying for our gasoline, groceries...) Second are core values. These are the few critical personal values we fully embrace and that, for us, have intrinsic worth. The benefit of aligning our life with our core values is the release of creativity and satisfaction. When these are released, our potential for living the *aware life* is maximized.

ORIGINAL INTENT

I believe we were created to be fully alive and fully connected to our soul, one another, and spiritually. Everyday life is far from utopia. Losses, longings never met, and disappointments, alter the original intent of life. Messy happens randomly and vicariously to the innocent and not so innocent, alike, as we all journey through this life.

The deep wounds in our subconscious come to life, and we behave and live from faulty thinking, leaving unrest and confusion. The heart responds with either anger and anxiety or apathy and coldness. In a nutshell, a wounded human being will respond with either rage or indifference. Either reaction brings destruction in relationships, careers, and personal fulfillment. Paula Rinehart, in her book, *Strong Women, Soft Hearts*, writes,

> If we can convince ourselves that we don't want, we won't hurt. For a while, at least. We can take the whole stinking mess, shove it in a closet, and lock the door. And then we convince ourselves that we no longer care. Of course, that defies all the laws of the heart.[5]

Because we all have a need to be loved and despite our best efforts feel our hurts deeply, this flawed world will wound us. These injuries might differ, but we as humans are all joined in this aspect of life—longing begets more longing. If needs and longings are unmet in childhood, children learn to separate from the wounding by disengaging from their emotions, others, or both. This pattern of emotional disengagement continues into adulthood. When we deaden or disown our desire through addictions, settling, or living out others' dreams, we miss the opportunity to live fully.

> *This is our 'pain point' - the moment we realize the pain of living this faulty, false life is more costly than our fear of change.*

The problem with the unconscious is that it is unconscious—that is until it starts to "show its hand" in our everyday life. This wounding often originates from the less minor damage of unmet needs to the most drastic wounding of abuse, neglect, abandonment, and unhealthy family systems.

Many of these wounds are rooted in the unconscious—far from awareness or knowledge. Thus, many psychological wounds go undetected until one day the ways of coping wear out. The destructive pathology wreaks havoc in our lives and the lives of loved ones. The alarm clock goes off in our psyches—it's our wake-up call telling us something is wrong, drastically wrong. And we can't ignore it any longer. It might be an unhealthy pattern in relationships, poor self-esteem, lousy self-care, or poor decision making that unmask our faulty thinking. This is our 'pain point' - the moment we realize the pain of living this faulty, false life is more costly than our fear of change. The desire to move away from this destructive pain is the greatest catalyst for change.

MESSY WOUNDS

I always had a sense of being slightly different from everyone else. Not quite fitting in. I felt like an "outsider" in my immediate family. As an extroverted child, I loved to sing and be silly. This behavior wasn't always at the most appropriate times. I would often burst into a song at the dinner table which was met with hushing and disdain. I learned quickly to hold my tune till I was alone at a later time. Often my chattiness as a child and extraversion were draining and disturbing to my more introverted family. Also, my parents were in grief much of my childhood due to the death of my older brother, Gary, who died at seven years old from complications of cerebral palsy and pneumonia. This grief and depression I see now, as an adult, was normal and healthy, but as a child left me feeling inadequate to make my parents happy.

Like all children, I so wanted to please my parents. When I felt I had failed; I concluded, "I wasn't enough." "I failed." "I was an outsider." Thus, my extroverted self was too much in the midst of the grief they were experiencing, and I felt it, deep inside. So, I started to work harder. I began to be the distraction from the grief. I developed the fine art of caretaking—if they needed nurture; I was kind and loving; if they needed to laugh—I was clown with a funny story. I became a chameleon to the needs of others. I lost myself trying to find a way to be an "insider."

I also struggled in school—I couldn't keep up with my schoolmates in reading or spelling. In third grade, I went through intelligence and academic testing and was ultimately diagnosed with dyslexia. My brother was always smart and achieved academically, but I was always put in the "C" reading group (which happened to be the lowest) and struggled to spell and pronounce words correctly. I was not confident in the classroom or with friends. So, I started to work harder...in things I could achieve, like athletics and friendships. But my inner struggle with learning was shameful to me and I felt I was an "outsider" both in my family and in the classroom.

The theme of being an "outsider" continued into my adult life. It showed up in many of the choices I made in adulthood. While most of my friends were having children, I wasn't. When most of my friends were getting married, I stayed single until I was thirty-six. The epitome of the being the outsider was when I married a man with four teenage children and became a stepmother. I was now part of a family unit, but it was the second squadron—the biological family was still strong and intact despite the divorce. I felt I was on the outside looking in.

I had not embraced my childhood wounds, and I continued this theme into my marriage. The feeling of being an "outsider" was familiar as I began living the role of being a stepmom. My husband, unknowingly, due to his guilt about his first divorce, was also unavailable to commit to me. The years of being overlooked took their toll on me, and I was the shell of the person I knew I was supposed to be.

Thus, even after counseling, I couldn't find myself or my joy in this marriage. We divorced and in response, I was separated from my community of friends and my church. And the life script continued. Until I recognized through therapy, workshops, and growth in my personal self-awareness that I indeed had a powerful life script ruling my life. The divorce was a tool in my self-awareness journey. Being an "outsider" was familiar and known. Continuing my life in this manner, I never had to embrace the pain inside. I never had to risk, trust, or commit.

I believe emotional injuries happen in life; they happen to all of us. Somewhere, somehow we are all going to get gashed open. Some of us experience the trauma of childhood abuse (sexual, physical, and emotional), neglect, hunger, divorce, or death of a loved one. While others have uneventful childhoods with the nice picket fence scenario and two adoring parents, but they will struggle too.

Wounds originate from a sense or feeling of not being enough, being unlovable, stupid, dirty, less than, different, an outsider, or unwanted. No matter what our childhood wound is - these wounds continue to influence each and every one of us. They impact the adult choices we make in relationships, careers, and life.

BEEN THERE DONE THAT

Personal psychological wounds need to be grappled with and understood to be healed. These wounds split our personality from true-self to form a false-self. The false-self develops for the purpose of emotional and psychological survival. Our psyche manufactures a false-self for the sheer purpose of defending the true-self from the threat of abandonment, criticism, harm, or failure. The false-self develops a pattern of beliefs and behaviors that enact when it perceives a similar threat. This faulty pattern influences us mentally, spiritually, and emotionally - limiting us from living up to our maximum potential. So, the question is not, "Do

I have a psychological wound?" but rather "Which psychological wound *do* I have?"

Psychological wounds are universal. This simply mean you and your loved ones are human and live in an imperfect world with other imperfect humans. These wounds are not in themselves mental illnesses, but they can cause faulty thought processes which result in damaging behaviors. Recent psychological research suggests that even "normal" or relatively "healthy" people have varying degrees of wounding. Thus, supporting the belief that life is messy and can psychologically injure indiscriminately.

Before I continue, please let me drive this truth home one more time—psychological wounding is universal. Thus, it does not warrant shame or guilt! The journey out of psychological wounds and subconsciously driven behavior is intentional self-awareness. It's this process of becoming more aware that leads to freedom, fulfillment, and the *aware life*.

Families are different in many ways, but one thing they have in common is that they exist to fulfill adult and children needs. Some families do this better than others. Depending on prior parenting examples, physical and mental health, and priorities of the adults, some families are more effective at nurturing needs of the family. Simply put—the ability to meet needs, especially children's needs, is largely due to the amount of nurturance the family can give.

Every family has a nurturance level, and it can range from low to high. And the level of nurture a child requires is unique to that child. So there are many variables which establish the degree of emotional health or injury each child experiences. These variables explain why one sibling describes their family as loving and supportive while their sister or brother describes the same family as harsh and demanding, or aloof and unresponsive. To nurture someone is to fill the needs of a living entity, but sometimes these needs go unmet or are under-met due to random difficulties and motives. So depending on how often all members' needs are fulfilled, a family would be described as somewhere between "low nurturance" and "high nurturance." Not surprisingly, it has been observed in a family with low nurture the most significant wounds appear. These include excessive fears, shame, and an inability to show care or have empathy for others.

TRIGGERS

We all can remember a word, tone, look, or situation that caused us to feel an intense emotion, usually a negative emotion. When this happens, we are triggered by an automatic response in such a way that is stronger or different from our usual manner. Our behavior might be so out of character that we don't even recognize ourselves. Flooded with rage, shame, sadness, or fear we act out to protect ourselves.

We unconsciously time travel back to the seed of the original wound—to the time when a deep hurt occurred and become overwhelmed with the intensity of emotion. We feel inundated with the fear of the abandonment, shame, or harm. And we react—feverishly. We feel out of control and behave in a destructive manner to protect and comfort our inner child. We feel criticized, unloved, alienated, lonely, numb, powerless, or unappreciated. We suddenly are saying and doing things that we know are not helpful or healthy, but we can't seem to stop. We are victims once again of our deep wound, and so we wound.

Here is a list of some of the more common triggers and responses. Have you ever felt this way?

- I felt judged, so I judged you.

- I felt flooded and didn't know what to do.

- I felt ashamed and made it your fault.
- I felt powerless, so I yelled or just became invisible.
- I felt lonely, so I found a way to get some attention.
- I felt belittled, so I got angry.

When we get triggered, we go back to a place in our life that we might or might not consciously remember. Our feelings are right back at the time of the initial trauma, but this time, as an adult, we can say and do things to protect ourselves. We can either let all the cannons loose—saying and doing all the things the inner child would've liked to have done in childhood. We spray an inadvertent chain of hurtful insults, name calling, and damage. Or we fade away into an invisible cloak, hoping not to be noticed as we sneak safely away. Whether it's a disagreement with our spouse, a belittling by our boss, or a misunderstanding with a friend, our reactions are extreme, to others and toward ourselves. We feel and respond much more intensely than the current situation warrants.

The false-self gets activated from a psychologically threatening event which allows the false-self to hijack the true-self—the wise part of our brain. When this happened, our thoughts, perceptions, and feelings are reincarnated to a prior wound or trauma. This reenactment of an earlier wound permits one of the false-self subselves (inner critic, shamed child, scared child, people pleaser, or procrastinator) to take control. The subself reacts to the real or perceived danger by seeking comfort in a familiar role and moves out of the true and authentic self.

The false-self disables the true-self and its ability to make wise long-term productive decisions. The short-sighted, comfort-seeking false-self who has taken over makes less wise and less healthy decisions—leaving messy and damaging repercussions.[6] It would be as if a Little League coach was trying to run a professional sports team. The fallout from the false-self leaves an array of damage, including broken relationships, job losses, and inner shame.

> *The false-self disables the true-self and its ability to make wise long-term productive decisions*

THE JOURNEY

I want everyone to know it's *possible* to mend wounds and change unhealthy patterns and find a life with more freedom, joy, and purpose. The journey of overcoming wounds has the possibility of healing people, families, groups, and communities through empathy and patience.

This journey will look different for each of us. We can shed our limiting ways of life and move forward with intentionality. The first step is exploring the messy parts of the past. Revisiting memories and wounds is not a place to get stuck; rather it's a place to begin.

As Nobel Prize in literature winner, André Gide wrote in 1925, "One doesn't discover new lands without consenting to lose sight, for a very long time, of the shore."[7] It is courage to embrace where we've been, so we can better understand how we got to where we are now.

> *"One doesn't discover new lands without consenting to lose sight, for a very long time, of the shore."*

MAKE MORE MISTAKES

Intentionality invites us to make more mistakes, take more risks, and feel more alive. Don't sit in the bleachers—dive in! If we feel trapped by the fear of failure, rejection, and loss, then it's our time to show up—jump in and take a risk. Life is calling out for change.

GET CURIOUS!

I see clients with a lot of internal fear. One of the characteristics of these type of people is they are usually judging and critical of others. They judge others because they are judging themselves. It is their coping mechanism to prevent the harsh thrashing they give their soul daily. If they actually get curious and look deep inside they might find a fantastic adventure waiting. That would release the shackles of lies they have endured for years. Be curious and don't judge. Find the freedom of not being controlled by fear or rejections. Give yourself permission to find you again.
The three keys to help everyone journey to a fulfilled *aware life* include:

TAKE RESPONSIBILITY!

Own your part! This journey is not a search and blame exploration. It's a journey to grow in understanding and taking personal responsibility for our choices, behaviors, and life. Which includes taking ownership for the hurt, chaos, and damage in our life and in the life of others.

GIVE UP CONTROL!

Control is just another way not to risk. If being out of control is terrifying, then this is one area to explore more diligently. Control issues typically come in two forms: the need to control how things get done or the need to control how others see us. Both forms require attention and change. So, to journey is to take risks and add some healthy exploration and adventure to our life.

GRACE!

Finally, give yourself grace. Don't demand perfection. Allow a little mess. Remember, we are all on a journey, and all journeys take time and grace. We are choosing to be awake and not sleep our life away. The intentional journey is a self-reflecting spiritual journey. We are entering sacred ground. Honor yourself as you gingerly embark on this deliberate path.

The journey to engage the soul in intentional living is our primary task. Engaging the soul will open up our world and free us from our own and others' expectations. The energy that emerges from this freedom is called love—the love of this life, this journey, and the love of healthy companionship on this journey. The soul cries out for freedom and love. So, dive in—get curious, give up control, and always, always, give yourself grace.

DISCOVERY DISCUSSION: **MESSY**

Recommendation: Do Exercise I - FULFILLMENT 30 PRE-TEST in Self-Awareness Exercises.

1. What does Messy Intentionality mean to you?

2. What core area/s of self-awareness do you recognize in your life that need growth?

   • Values

   • Emotional Needs

   • Lifestyle

   • Emotional Awareness

3. Did you identify any triggers in your life?

4. Anne Lamott says, "There is ecstasy in paying attention." What does that mean to you in your own words?

5. The false-self can be very powerful in one's life. Are there areas in your life you feel you are not being true to yourself?

6. Do you know where you have unresolved wounds in your life? (Share them with the group or write them down—so you can come back to them later.)

7. What area/s in your life would you like to see change?

CHAPTER 2

LONGING

Longing is a strange animal. It lies at the center of all things. Longing can bring us into the safe and secure arms of those we love, but sometimes, when not acknowledged and honored, it can send us over the edge of the proverbial cliff.

We long for belonging, meaning, purpose, and connection. The heart is a collection of longings and desires that can be as dangerous as they are exhilarating. It is profound to realize the true language of the heart is the language of desire. The journey to understand and fulfill our longings must be walked with patience and with strength. If we avoid this walk, we chance staying at the very place we are today for the rest of our life. To journey is to find our life's ultimate satisfaction and completeness, to wholly know who we are without any mechanism of protection. Only with our defenses down can our true-self emerge.

Through the years, as I have counseled thousands of people who are trying to have a more fulfilled life, I have learned that the very thing they are searching for can be found within themselves just by asking one simple question. "Am I ready to become something else, something better?" This is the pivotal point of the journey.

Kara was one of my first clients in whom I recognized this process was aching to begin. Kara's life was cast in characters of aloof relationships, dependency, and addictions. "I want to know me again," she stated. "I want to laugh again." Her desire for laughter was a cry for connection. Behind her attempts to dull her pain was a longing for intimacy. She had moved away from friends and family, and was in a marriage that lacked connection not to mention passion. Kara was encased in resentment and longing. She didn't know how she could find herself again. "I did what I thought I was supposed to do, but I feel so lost." Somewhere along the way, Kara's image of herself became lost, and a facade or false-self presented itself. Kara knowing she could no longer live feeling like she was just existing and not living—courageously began her journey of self-discovery.

We all come to a place where our false-self encounters the threat of exposure. Some choose to be intentional and journey; some choose to stay in the habitual path of least resistance.

TRUE-SELF

In my work as a coach and counselor, I have found that experiences of loss, shame, hurt, and loneliness alter an individual's self-image. They diminish creativity and individuality, producing a false-self. These emotional wounds alter the genuine self and introduce a more defensive self—which doesn't risk exposing the true, authentic person. Ultimately, the true-self hides behind a mask. The false self protects from the possibility of rejection, conflict, non-acceptance, and anger. Thus, the emergence of a facade or a veneer and plastic self.

> *Living a life that is not true to ourself*
> *is actually death to our soul.*

With time, we will begin to notice our false-self will fiercely block our efforts to honor our true-self. The false self does not desire the emergence of our true-self. The false-self is king, and true-self emergence threatens its power. Living a life that is not true to ourself is actually death to our soul. It takes the very nature of who we are and turns us into the "appropriate" person we believe others want us to be. The true-self fades into darkness, peeking, on occasion, around the corner. It is the returning from the protective and unaware life, deadened and lifeless, into real living that makes our heart celebrate and feel energy again. The path to this redemption can be challenging and hurtful, but it is absolutely necessary.

Kara, my client, recognized the adaptation she had performed to meet others' expectations and after a lot of self-discovery work started living a more aware and intentional life. She stopped pretending she was happy when inside she was dying. In working with my clients, I find fear of failure, fear of disappointment, and/or fear of the unknown to be the greatest hindrances to change. Overcoming these fears starts with self-awareness and commences in living our true identity. Kara stated, "I am living the life that is right for me and for those I love, because for the first time in my life I'm being real." Kara's decision to pursue a truer image of herself than the one she had been living was the foundation for finding her true-self and living a more fulfilled life.

FIND YOUR OWN LIFE—STOP BORROWING MINE

Self-confidence is built on a deep sense of knowing and accepting ourself. I believe the keys to a fulfilled *aware life* are optimism, humility, forgiveness, and gratitude. The person who lives being fully present and aware has these pillars present and active in all aspects of their life. Living in such a way produces deep contentment in spite of what life may bring. And life is so much more when it is lived genuinely.

The act of being intentional begins with becoming conscious of our emotions and desires every moment. If we do not reflect on our life and the things that brought us to the present, then the same patterns will continue to work their way toward unconscious replication. It is important to identify the mysterious current that carries us forward, toward what was intended for our life. And likewise to be aware of the social, religious, and familial forces that may have a subconscious influence.

Recovering our purpose also starts with taking responsibility for our life. Stop blaming others for our disappointments, even if others have intentionally hurt us. We are the ones who now has the power to make the choices for our life. When we begin to reflect on the patterns of the past, then we begin to work from a place of self-awareness. Ask yourself, "Whose life have I been living anyway?" If it is not yours, whose life is it? In many cases, people live the unlived lives of parents, grandparents, or authority figures. Living to satisfy some unmet need in a family member's life can repeat unhealthy patterns and manifest in behaviors such as denial, minimization, rationalization, or various addictions.

Søren Kierkegaard, nineteenth century Danish philosopher, said: "Life can only be understood backwards; but it must lived forwards."[1]

> *"Life can only be understood backwards;*
> *but it must lived forwards."*

Even when things are going well, sometimes life just doesn't feel as good as you think it should. Our lives are giving us clues that we often miss—clues found in the choices we make, regarding relationships, jobs, etc. However, they are often buried in internalized messages such as: "Make money." "Get married." "Have children." "Choose security over truth." "Choose what others are choosing."

These messages become foundations we use to gain love, success, security, approval, and a sense of community. So why, then, do they not deliver such results? Why does the hum of indifference come to the surface—the restless nights, the temptation of an illicit relationship, addictions to people, alcohol, drugs, and sex? Do we pursue these things for comfort or numbness?

Could these symptoms light the path to what we seek? Personal purpose and fulfillment is found in walking away from the definitive statements of others and finding the "fit" for *your* life. Examining the messages that once promised fulfillment might be our greatest clue to our personal self-awareness and toward living the life we desire. We may discover which values our soul has been carrying with the hopes that one day we would align our life with *those* values. What does it profit to gain the world and find that the price is loss of relationship to our soul? In journeying through the swamplands of disappointment and loss, our real self is reclaimed. It is found in experiencing our own disappointments as well as embracing others.

The bad news for those who choose the path of pursuing our real life is that there may be suffering and loss at the beginning. The truth is, however, we likely will suffer regardless of which road we take—whether that suffering be in the form of reclaiming our lost dreams and passions or in the loss of our true-self.

Why are we so afraid to suffer? Suffering can bring rich meaning and direction in our lives. So often I have seen clients who knew what they were called to do and what decisions they should make, but they were paralyzed by the possibility of rejection, abandonment, and the fear of growing up to be totally responsible for themselves. The soul itself has brought us to a difficult place to enlarge us, to ask more of us, to cause change. There is something within us that pulls us toward our real self, as there is also something that seeks the comfortable and the familiar. Growth demands facing fear; however, we reactively learn patterns that protect against such growth.

In James Hollis's book *Finding Meaning in the Second Half of Life* he states, "If we cannot speak the truth, our truth, to ourselves, we will be unable to speak it to the world either."[2] The psyche at work manifests in the presence of suffering. The soul itself has brought us to a difficult place to enlarge us, to ask more of us, to cause us to grow and change.

> *"If we cannot speak the truth, our truth, to ourselves, we will be unable to speak it to the world either."*

SHAME

Unmet and disparaged desires for intimacy and connection breed an artificial manner of relating to others, the world, and even to our self. Shame is a significant negative force in the journey of intentional living. Psychologist and author, Dr. Brené Brown, defines shame as "an intensely painful feeling or experience of believing we are flawed and therefore unworthy of acceptance and belonging. Shame creates feelings of fear, blame and disconnection."[3]

Shame is an emotion that combines feelings of dishonor, unworthiness, and embarrassment. It's a bad feeling that most of us will go to great lengths to avoid. It can arise suddenly and unexpectedly, or it may be a pervasive feeling that one feels all the time. It is usually not founded on any single action but, rather, it is founded on the expectations of others. More precisely, its roots are grounded in the perception of having failed another's expectation. Guilt is different from shame because guilt comes from an actual breach of internal values. Many times shame will follow guilt, but shame can stand alone, wreaking havoc on our soul, our relationships, and our health.

Shame is a believed violation of cultural or social standards. We feel that we are unusual in some way or that our desires are too much or too different. It comes from feeling that parents, teachers, or even God does not accept us. It can come later in life from other authority figures like bosses and even spouses. Shame attacks our longings. It turns us away from being authentic and honest. Shame peeks its head out when the real or perceived fear of rejection is anticipated. We learn how to safely hide our desires, to live a façade, all to avoid the pain of feeling shame.

Shame is real pain. It is not made up or imaginary. It is fiercely alive in all of us. Dr. Brené Brown, in her book *Daring Greatly*, says the first three things we need to know about shame are the following:

1. We all have it. Shame is universal and one of the most primitive human emotions we experience. The only people who don't experience shame lack the capacity for empathy and human connection.

2. We're all afraid to talk about shame.

3. The less we talk about shame, the more control it has over our lives.[4]

A powerful discovery is made at some point in childhood that we can maneuver the truth about who we really are. Often shame begins with the fear of disconnection. All people are hardwired for connection. As I previously stated, shame goes quickly to the core of who we are—it is the fear that something we've done or failed to do makes us unlovable or worthy of belonging. From that simple fear, the groundwork for the development of the false-self is laid. In essence, we learn to pretend to prevent the feeling of shame. We develop an identity that is accepted and validated by the significant people in our life. We learn that even if we are sad, we can appear to be happy, or if we are afraid, we can exhibit bravery.

We show our best impression to maintain our self-esteem. Yet, inside we feel wrong, unacceptable, and "other." So we learn to live behind masks. Gradually, these masks become our identity. And our identity is not just in how we want others to see us, but over time, they reflect how we want to see ourselves. We have lost our real self and assumed an identity based on illusion.

●

Mark was the type of young man who everyone loved to be around. He was well known and liked in the community. Despite his gregarious and fun loving personality, he struggled with who he was. To everyone on the outside, Mark's family was a close, supportive, and loving family. His parents were well-educated and prestigious in the Christian community in which they associated. No one would have known Mark's deep sense of anguish and shame. He kept his true-self tucked far away. His desire to be true to himself was suffocated by the longing to please his family and live up to the expectations of the community. He was engaged to a woman he wasn't in love with and pursuing a career in the footsteps of his father. Mark wanted neither.

Inadequacy and the fear of failure ultimately manifested into severe depression and sexual addictions, to the point that Mark tried to take his life. Fortunately, he was unsuccessful. The next day, as Mark and I talked, he began the long therapeutic process of unraveling the facades of his life. He understood that the unhealthy attachments he had made to his false-self were ways of coping with vulnerability, shame, and inadequacy. Mark changed his career goals and broke off his engagement. He started to live a genuine lifestyle and vocation. His parents were displeased, but grew to accept Mark as he was, and most importantly he accepted his true-self.

MISPLACED LONGING

Another way of suppressing our true-self is placing our energies from true longing into artificial means of coping in order to fill the void inside. Misplaced longings can come out in addictions or in other means of satisfying healthy desires in an unhealthy way. The end result is getting too much of something, even if that something is good in moderation. An addiction crosses the line from enjoyment to abuse. We become addicted to a relationship, substance, sexual pleasure, or an identity. An addiction or attachment is our desire to be dependent on or attached to a specific object or person in an unhealthy manner.

What we do with the experience of pain establishes—in a significant part—the way we behave, think, and relate. It can either hugely boost the passions of our heart to the point addictive behaviors are evident or diminish and alter our passions, making them more acceptable and palatable to others' expectations. Our hearts are made to be passionate. We are born with many passions, beginning with simple longings as babies that grow and become more complicated with time. We still long for something or someone to tell us we are of value and worth. When those longings are met with indifference, we often become ambivalent to our passions, discounting them, as we disconnect from our passions. When we deaden our desire, Paula Rinehart, in her book *Strong Women, Soft Hearts*, writes, the following things occur:

- We don't have to face the disappointment of a lost dream.

- We save ourselves from doing the slow and tedious work of repairing a broken relationship.

- We don't have to sit patiently—or not so patiently—with the things we don't understand.

- And we can avoid, a little longer, our fear of what others will think.[5]

BE GENTLE WITH YOURSELF

Self-deception occurs automatically when our real self is not embraced. As psychologist and theologian David G. Benner states:

> …[Self-deception is] part of what psychologists mean when they say that the defense mechanisms operate in the unconscious. It is also part of what theologians mean when they speak of original sin. We don't really have to choose self-deception. It is—to use contemporary computer jargon—the default option.[6]

The *aware life* starts with self-awareness and self-empathy. It starts with accepting our longings, failures, and limited vision. It is completely counter opposite to what Benner calls the "default" option. Self-empathy allows us to be gentle with ourselves as we move intentionally toward our true-self. Awareness of our feelings will guide us to be honest and true to ourself.

The wonderment of self-empathy is that we allow ourselves to be flawed. When we allow ourselves to make mistakes and give ourselves grace, we are developing self-empathy. We then naturally apply the emotional intelligence skill of empathy in our relationships. The goal of focusing on self and self-empathy is not ultimately to breed narcissism, producing people who only want their pleasure in this life; rather, it is to bring out compassion and kindness. As self-empathy increases, the skills that allow us to detect others' feelings and respond to them wisely will change our interactions. We become more peaceful, genuine, and centered. Self-empathy leads us to act honestly, kindly, selflessly, and bravely toward others.

JOE

Joe came to my office with significant and pervasive symptoms of depression. He was married and had three children. Parenting was a struggle, and one of his stepsons was especially a challenge for him. He just couldn't seem to connect with him as he did with the other children. This caused tension and fed the progressing estranged relationship he had with his wife. His marriage was dull, and he and his wife looked more like roommates with chores than a married couple. Joe was struggling at his workplace with multiple absences, and when he did go to the office, his lack of concentration made him irritable and ineffective. He eventually lost his job, which compounded his depression.

Joe came to counseling looking for help, and he admitted he didn't know what else to do. He found himself stuck and neck deep in hopelessness. I saw him for six months, and his depression showed little improvement, yet he was consistent in making his appointments. I was beginning to wonder what I needed to do next in his treatment. He was on an antidepressant. I had used an eclectic approach to his therapy, but nothing seemed to help. I continued to feel like I was missing a piece in the puzzle. I probed for answers to deeper issues and came up with very little that could explain his significant depression.

Then one day after a particularly difficult session, Joe called me. "I need to talk to you again." "Can I come back in this week?" His voice was intense, and an overtone of nervousness was detectable. The previous appointment I had invited his wife to join the session. Now he wanted an appointment to be alone. I made time for him, and we met. Joe stated, "I have never told anyone this." I paused and reassured him again that everything mentioned in session would remain confidential. He struggled and took a deep breath. "Ever since I was aware of any sexual feelings, I have been confused." Already sensing where he was going with this information, I felt a mixture of excitement that he was choosing to allow truth to illuminate the struggle that he had lived with for so long. He was speaking for the first time in his life with honesty and courage, acknowledging his struggle with same-sex attraction. The reality of what he had to do for all those years to abate his fear of being found out in his conservative community was overwhelming. The realization that he had been alone without someone to walk with him through his confusion struck me with intense sadness. I waited silently knowing he needed to say the words...his words of his struggle.

Finally, he said. "I'm gay." I paused and let the reality of his words soak in. I gently smiled and hopefully comforted his fears. I told him I was proud of him for finally speaking out loud the words he had said a thousand times in his head. I reassured him it was courageous and healthy to acknowledge finally the sexual struggle, which he viciously tried to hide for years. I also let him know I believed we could deal more effectively with his depression. The guilt and shame he had over his inner confusion and porn addiction collided with his religious upbringing. He was held captive. Joe stated, "I went into my own box—being non-emotional, disconnected, dispassionate—because I was afraid someone would see my biggest secret. Someone would see that I'm gay."

Others' expectations of Joe had suppressed his ability to be true to himself and others. But now, with honesty, Joe could begin the journey toward understanding his feelings and finding truth for his life—based on his longings and desires. He started to reclaim his desire to be known and accepted by the people in his life. Thus we began in therapy the journey together of what it meant for Joe to align his life with his beliefs, his values, and his sexuality.

WAKE UP!

When we find the place in our life where we know we belong, we are truly living. We engage the world with our mask off and implementing the four pillars of the *aware life:* optimism, humility, forgiveness, and gratitude. This fullness of life is found in the journey of going deeper into our soul and then getting emotionally "naked" with a few close people in our life. Waking up to our life begins in the arena of self-acceptance. Until we are willing to accept the unpleasant truths of our life, we will rationalize or deny responsibility for our unhealthy and even damaging behavior. Freedom to allow our heart to accept our longings comes with self-acceptance from asking the harder questions—and taking responsibility with the answers we find. A radical encounter with truth is the only thing powerful enough to unmask the illusions of the false-self.

Brent Curtis and John Eldredge capture the importance of living from the heart in their book *The Sacred Romance*. They write,

In the end, it doesn't matter how well we have performed or what we have accomplished—a life without heart is not worth living. For out of this wellspring of our soul flow all true caring and all meaningful work, all real worship and all sacrifice.[7]

Living life wholehearted allows the longing for meaning to be evident in all we do and all we are.

Living life wholehearted allows the longing for meaning to be evident in all we do and all we are. This is waking up to our intentional self-aware life. This is an enlarged life—the *aware life*.

DISCOVERY QUESTIONS: LONGING

Recommendation: Do Exercise II - *THE AWARE LIFE FULFILLMENT SCALE* in Self-Awareness Exercises.

1. What does *longing* mean to you?

2. To awaken your true-self, you must acknowledge any defense mechanism and false identity you have formed.

    i. What roadblocks do you think you may encounter as you pursue self-awareness and possible change?

    ii. What are the components of your false self?

3. Søren Kierkegaard penned, *"Life can only be understood backwards; but it must lived forwards."* Look back over your life - what do you understand about yourself that you didn't before?

4. What keeps you from allowing others to know your true-self? Discuss….

5. What is self-empathy? What is self-empathy's role in living an intentional life?

CHAPTER 3

LOSSES

The phone rings with unexpected news of a car accident, a death, a loss. The test results are confirmed that indeed it is cancer, disease, infertility. The divorce papers are delivered, and so the story is told—a story of loss and pain and of disillusionment and confusion. Life indeed is messy! Everyone has a story, but many of us forget to tell ours. We forget there is a beginning and an ending that belongs just to us. Often stories are fragmented pieces that are tossed into the mixture of what makes up life, never to find meaning and connection. The essence of the story gets lost in a chaotic concoction of disguise. When we choose to tell our stories, their worth, passion, and meaning are celebrated through the telling.

Loss can be the beginning of a journey, or—to phrase it more accurately—it can be the happening that awakens us to our journey—if we so choose. We can be intentional and choose to process our loss. Alternatively, we can stay asleep and allow loss to suffocate our dreams and passions. I have done both. I have buried my pain so deeply that I wasn't even conscious of its power my decisions and relationships. I tried to repress it, but it never disappeared. Loss and pain remained hidden my subconscious, waiting to inject fear in my heart, havoc in my life, and doubt in myself. I remembered a word of wisdom once given to me: A memory with strong emotional connection can never be buried. If buried, it is always buried alive and waits for the next time something triggers the memory. And, when triggered, the emotion comes back with a vengeance. It is armed and ready to destroy love, relationships, and one's concept of self. This is what happened to me.

GOOD-BYES

My mother passed away when I was in my mid-thirties. No matter what age you are, you're never quite ready to say good-bye to your mom. My mother's story is one of mishaps and questions. Her diagnosis was straightforward: colon cancer. The treatment was not. It was harsh and invasive. In the end, the sequela of her cancer "treatment", not cancer itself, caused my mother's death. My dad, brother, and I all anticipated the typical nausea hair loss, weight loss, and skin burn from the radiation, but we were not prepared for losing her. After months of treatment, the assessment from the doctors signaled all clear, meaning the cancer was gone. We thought she would start feeling better, gain weight, and be Mom again. We waited, and, more importantly, *she* waited. We waited for healing.

But the healing never came. I watched her, and I remember my feelings of helplessness—which were smothered by feelings of guilt and shame. As a registered nurse, I felt I should have known more about her treatment. I should have pushed for a second opinion and even opted for a treatment that was less invasive and damaging to her colon. I should've known more. I should've done more. The "should haves" had been very powerful in my life previously, and once again they came back full force. Along with the "should haves" came guilt. Guilt became too familiar. I felt I could have done better, that I should have been perfect. I never allowed for my human faults; there wasn't room. *Should have* kept me on my toes and performing.

My mother kept losing weight and feeling fatigued and weak. The treatment had damaged her colon tissue and made it so fragile that it couldn't pass fecal matter. This left my mom susceptible to perforation and, consequentially, possible sepsis (severe infection). I remember the long walks in the hospital hall with my mom, trying to promote her colon to work properly. Her body was fragile, and yet, with determined strength, she walked. She walked slowly, but she walked.

During this time in the hospital, I was embracing my mother's mortality—in addition to embracing my separation and dependence from her. It was an ironic moment when I experienced the tug of war between dependency and independence. My true-self was not present. I was distant from what was real because being real was much too scary and much too… well, real. I spoke in sentences that did not allow anyone a glimpse into my soul. I searched for the place in-between showing enough vulnerability, but not breaking my emotional veneer to show my heart was breaking. Strength with a smidgen of humanity gave the illusion of realness. It was all I could do at that time.

My mother, later that week, suffered from abdominal perforation that allowed bacteria-filled fluid to seep outside her bowels and catapulted her boy into the dreaded sepsis. She was rushed into surgery with the goal of closing the perforation while giving her a high-dose antibiotic to fight the infection. That was the last time I saw my mom awake and coherent. She went into a coma and never woke again. We sat at her side for weeks while she was intubated and non-responsive.

Friends and family came to visit, to pray, to sing to her, and to sit with us. There were times I saw her eyes follow mine. I knew she was there, but I wasn't sure how much she understood. One day my future husband came to visit my mom and asked for her blessing on my upcoming wedding—the wedding she would never attend. At that moment, her eyes looked directly at him and blinked, and her hand squeezed his. I knew my mom was struggling to communicate with us, using a body that no longer responded. Weeks later, she passed away.

It has taken years to thaw out the frozen fraction of my heart that the loss of my mom shaped. It took a while to grieve fully and to start accepting this loss. I still miss her and always will, but losing her does not keep me held in a place grief and loss anymore. Fifteen years later, I lost my father in a very similar way. Even in my fifties, the loss of both parents left awkwardly lost, and a deep levels of emotions emerged, opening up a new journey into self-awareness. With every loss is a door to self-awareness—if we choose to open it and process all that is within.

NECESSARY LOSSES

Life is a journey through many different losses. To live the intentional *aware life*, they must be recognized. Judith Viorst authored a book called *Necessary Losses: The Loves, Illusions, Dependencies, and Impossible Expectations That All of Us Have to Give Up in Order to Grow*. In these pages, she fleshes out her primary concept of loss being a necessary part of life. The bond between loss and gain is fundamental to living a full and successful life. She stresses that loss is a far more encompassing theme than just death. As she explains in her book, loss embraces not just leaving and being left but also change, moving on, and letting go. Wisdom comes with realizing what we must give up, willingly or unwillingly, to grow.[1] Change is a vital part of life. If we are one of the few who embraces change, then we may not see it so evidently as loss. But for those who fight and scream to keep everything the same, change is a huge hurdle to overcome or avoid at all cost.

Embracing loss allows for growth. Changing a life pattern can bring wonderful new things, but the desire to maintain familiarity runs deep. It's not until what we think is normal becomes too boring or damaging that we start to accept the uncomfortable feelings that accompany change.

Pursuing our personal fulfillment will often bring about change, possibly a great amount. This change might alter relationships and careers. It might alter the way we have always lived our life. Boundaries may need to be redefined. Some relationships may need healthy closure while for others the door is opened further. Careers might be redirected and new ones embarked upon. Pursuing fulfillment takes courage and stamina as well as incredible risk. But when we are journeying forward and getting closer to our passion - energy and excitement become our constant companions.

SITTING WITH THE UNKNOWN

Learning to sit with the unknown is fundamental in the process of finding gains in losses. The tendency to run from or minimize the impact of loss can drastically interfere with growth and healing. The ability to "sit with the unknown" could be defined as ambivalence with a purpose. It is feeling the pain of loss, betrayal, and failure without running back to numbing, familiar patterns. It is learning how to rest in the pain until something better emerges. In the meantime having safe people who let us share our struggles and "own" our pain is key. Owning our pain means being aware and honest about our hurts without the expectation of others healing us. We must be able to share our pain for the sake of growth and healing.

It is learning how to rest in the pain until something better emerges.

In my counseling practice, I typically have two types of clients when it comes to dealing with loss in a negative manner. The first are those individuals who are stuck in a painful memory and can't see their life rich and fulfilled again. They typically suffer from depression and struggle because they lack the energy for things they used to enjoy. These individuals need help getting unstuck so they can start their journey of healing. The second are those who do everything they can to avoid dealing with the consequences of pain and loss. They numb their feeling and live in a bubble of denial and minimization.

Often people would rather continue living their lives in monotony as they slide across the surface of reality. There is incongruence between how they desire their lives to be and the choices they make that leave them stuck. Processing loss is seen as too excruciating, and many choose never to embrace this challenging journey. Loss can be the jump-start to a new life—that is if we choose to let its full power turn our life around.

READY FOR CHANGE?

Steve, a client, is a good example of someone who chose to deal with pain by denying its very existence. Steve was an alcoholic, a gambler with no limits, and an addict of conquests in sexual relationships. These were his tools of denial. He did everything he could to avoid the full power of change from his destructive behaviors. He ran far from the haunting memories of being raised by a physically abusive father and an emotionally neglectful mother. Steve's life had been lived between episodes of pain and misuse. His identity was hidden in shame and failure. He learned to numb the pain from his past with addictions.

Steve was on his third marriage when I met him. He had been unsuccessful in two prior marriages, and the pattern of failure was continuing in his present relationship. He began his first session by listing everything that was wrong with wife number three.

When I work with clients like Steve in my therapy practice, I have come to appreciate the categorizing of clients outlined in *Solution-Focused Therapy*.[2] These identifiers help me, as a therapist, know what I can and cannot do for my clients and how best to help them heal.

The first category is the *visitor*, one who comes into an appointment just to check it out. There is nothing wrong with this scenario. In this case, the potential clients are seeing if therapy is really for them, or, more accurately, if I (the therapist) am the one they are going to trust to help them along the journey. Some are ready to trust; some are not.

The second category is the *complainer*. (This one isn't hard to figure out.) This type of client is easy for me to identity - I can feel my energy drain with every negative and blaming word they speak. They are there to have someone agree that everything and everyone in their life downright sucks. Clients in this category, are not invested in growth or change, they are stuck and have no desire to change. While some of my clients start off in this category they quickly advance to a healthier stage, due primarily to the power of empathetic listening. I find that clients cannot stay in this place for long. Soon after beginning counseling, they are either ready to move into the next category, or they leave therapy, unaffected. This is where Steve was, but I had high hopes that, in time, he would move into becoming a customer—one who wanted to be true to his authentic self.

The *customer* or what I like to call the *journeyer* is the last category. This is the individual ready to work, ready to buy in, ready to journey. As I mentioned before, telling our story is freeing in itself. Sharing it with another person and receiving empathy can be powerfully healing. Much of the therapy and coaching is helping the client tell their story. The simple act of telling our story allows the narrative to take form. The listener (therapist or coach) then can clarify the story by asking questions that draw out missing pieces or forgotten parts. Thus, self-awareness is sparked, and understanding and change can occur.

I began to have hope for Steve's journey as I saw his complaining nature morph into the real emotion of sadness. He told his story—the joys and the hurts. Over the next few months, I was granted glimpses into his soul. He was starting to feel safe enough to be real with me and real with himself. He was beginning to own his part of the relationship troubles and his addictions. He took responsibility to start the process of change and stopped his destructive patterns and started to believe he had worth and value. Steve's change was fully dependent on identifying the lies he believed about himself and replaced them with healthy and loving truths.

Being raised by a mother that was always finding fault with what he did, embedded the faulty message that Steve wasn't good enough. If Steve brought a "B" home from school, she would ask, "Why not an A?", or when mowing the yard, she would only comment on how one part of it was uneven. Her subtle manipulative comments of disapproval wrecked havoc on Steve's self-esteem. Everything he did was met with criticism. She could never be pleased. Though he tried to satisfy his mother, he was rarely successful. He developed a protected self that vowed never to be criticized again. Steve brought this defense to his marriages and with every disagreement or difference of opinion, he would hear criticism. He would lash out at any comment that he perceived was criticism in an attempt to preserve his self-esteem. Ultimately, this led to him losing his first two marriages and nearly his third.

Steve began to see in the therapy sessions how his defensive reactions stemmed from his mother's critical words. Correcting the lies of inadequacy Steve had developed in childhood, and then he was able to take responsibility for his behavior as an adult. Steve faced the truth, and he faced loss – the loss of never receiving the validation from his mother that he so desired. With his true identity being restored he was able to manage his angry outbursts and defensiveness. Steve viewed his wife from a different lens—fostering a deeper, safer, and fulfilling relationship.

BECOMING REAL

I believe the greatest analogy of becoming real is captured in a wonderful children's book called *The Velveteen Rabbit* by Margery Williams. Toni Raiten-D'Antonio captures the adult message of this book in *The Velveteen Principles*. In the children's book, the main characters teach us how to find the peace that comes when we focus on what matters most in life: love, relationships, and empathy for ourselves and others. In the following passage from Williams's book, a stuffed animal called the Velveteen Rabbit asks another wiser toy, the Skin Horse, what it means to be real:

> "What is REAL?" asked the Rabbit one day, when they were lying side by side near the nursery fender, before Nana came to tidy the room. "Does it mean having things that buzz inside you and a stick-out handle?"
> "Real isn't how you are made," said the Skin Horse. "It's a thing that happens to you. When a child loves you for a long, long time not just to play, but REALLY loves you, then you become Real."
> "Does it hurt?" asked the Rabbit.
> Sometimes," said the Skin Horse, for he was always truthful. "When you are Real you don't mind being hurt."
> "Does it happen all at once, like being wound up," he asked, "or bit by bit?"

"It doesn't happen all at once," said the Skin Horse. "It takes a long time. That's why it doesn't happen to people who break easily, or have sharp edges or who have to be carefully kept. Generally, by the time you are Real, most of your hair has been loved off, and your eyes drop out and you get loose in the joints and very shabby. But those things don't matter at all, because once you are Real you can't be ugly, except to people who don't understand." [3]

To be real, to be emotionally conscious, sometimes involves losing things we never thought we would be able to live without. And in their place, finding value, worth, and purpose. The quest for the *aware life* can be found many times in the awakening of our soul through loss.

GRIEVING WELL

Grief is the catalyst to self-exploration, expression, and eventually freedom. I believe if we have lived at least twenty years on this planet—probably less—we all have something to grieve. Perhaps there's a dream that we realized would never come to fruition, a relationship lost, or a loved one's death. We may have experienced the demise of who we thought we were, or maybe we've experienced the dying fantasy of who we thought others were. You have forfeited these dreams for the more diminished and realistic view. We must grieve. To grow—to have real connection with ourself and others —we must grieve.

At thirty-six, Cindy was delighted to find out she was pregnant. She and her husband, Tom, had been trying to conceive for three years. The news was met with great expectations. But around thirty weeks into the pregnancy things changed drastically. A concerned Cindy called Tom and told him, "I'm having severe pain and cramping." They decided she should call the doctor. The doctor was unalarmed and told her to wait and rest to see if the pain went away. This being their first child and not knowing what to expect, they took the advice of the doctor and waited. Cindy's pain increased - and so did her anxiety. She knew intuitively something was wrong. Tom made the decision to go to the emergency room. At the hospital, they were immediately taken for an emergency C-section. Kelly, their daughter, was not breathing on her own at birth and was rushed to the neonatal intensive care unit—where she stayed for the next eight weeks.

When Kelly was ten months old, her pediatrician identified marked developmental issues. A year later, Kelly was officially diagnosed with mild mental retardation and cerebral palsy from the lack of oxygen at birth. Cindy who was struggling with sadness, guilt, and anger called my office in search of help. When Cindy came for her first appointment, she appeared as someone who had it all together. She was beautiful, intelligent, and confident - yet looking into her eyes, they revealed a very different story. Cindy's outer veneer was starting to crack. She began to tell her story, and I saw her sorrow in every tear that dropped.

Healing often begins by telling our story to someone who cares and shows empathy. It can be a friend, counselor, or coach, but it needs to be said. It is vital to the self-awareness journey. It facilitates the subconscious into awareness—as we pay close attention to our words and emotions as our narrative is unfolding.

In session, Cindy started to explore her grief. At one point, she admitted how she had questioned her bonding to her own daughter. "I felt like she was not my child," she admitted. Cindy had dreamed for years of all the things she would do with her daughter. The dream had to be altered. She had to face her disappointment and her shame. When she finally allowed herself to grieve without shame or guilt, Cindy's protective veneer began to melt. She was able to bond and dream of mother-daughter adventures she would have with Kelly. They were different from the original dreams, but with time became even more precious to her. Cindy experienced joy again. "I'm allowing myself acceptance and forgiveness, and learning to love Kelly in a way I never have before."

SECOND CHANCES

In my early forties, the built-up resentment I felt in my pleasing, caretaking, passive way of relating was starting to take a toll on me. I found myself angry, bitter, and desiring to break away from all those who took advantage of the pleaser in me. This side of me was unhealthy and not aligned with my real self. Pleasers are typically people who do most anything to make everyone else happy at the expense of their own wants, desires, and needs. With time, the stress from this type of behavior has destructive results physically, emotionally, and behaviorally.

This is when I found the heart to write my first book; *Finding Me Again: A Journey to an Authentic Life*, even though I was terribly afraid of the vulnerability it demanded. I needed to take a path that forced me to look squarely in the mirror and see my failures (real and perceived), my fears, and my successes. During this time it was difficult to accept and admit my imperfections. I saw so much I wanted and needed to change. I saw a woman who was just discovering who she was and who regretted many of the past decisions in her life. I didn't even recognize the face in the mirror. The woman staring back at me was not known. I could not recognize myself - I was so far from my authentic self.

There were moments I wondered if it would have been best to continue down the road I had been walking, the path of what others expected. The road would have brought less conflict and disruption to my life. But I knew something big needed to change. Weighing all this was the beginning of my discovery process. I mustered the courage to ask myself, *What do I need in order to accept myself—good, bad, and ugly? What do I need to recognize that is not me but, instead, what I have allowed myself to become in light of what others expected me to be?*

Jungian psychology would deduce much of what I was experiencing was the dichotomy between social conventions and my true-self. Parents, friends, church authorities, and media told me directly and indirectly who I was supposed to be, but those expectations clashed with who I was. The "safe" self would adhere to the expectations of others, living a status-quo life, but it wasn't working for me.

Stress from destructive ways of relating can do severe damage in our life and in the life of others. When we acknowledge the parts of ourself that need growth, we then have a second chance for a new life, a fuller life. Being intentional to become self-aware, acknowledge this awareness, and choose to grow is the beginning of our second chance in life. It was for me. Becoming real can be painful, but it becomes a gift when the joy of living a self-aware life is revealed.

> *Being intentional to become self-aware, acknowledge this awareness, and choose to grow is the beginning of our second chance in life.*

MESSY RELATIONSHIPS

A large percentage of my private practice involves relationship coaching and counseling. Every couple comes into my office with complex issues. Thus, the finding of solutions is often complicated.

The teeter-totter is an analogy I use when I work with couples. Probably all of us have a memory of going up and down on a teeter-totter with a friend on the grade school playground. We always tried to even the weight on each side so it would flow easily up and down. If one person were much bigger than the other, the smaller person would have to work hard pushing up with her legs, making the whole teeter-totter experience not so fun. Well, relationships are often like this—heavy on one end and not flowing rhythmically like we had expected it too.

When we figuratively see our relationships not waxing and waning in harmonious rhythm, we become aware that the relationship is off kilter and is need of repair. The couple must acknowledge the relationship is struggling, just like the unbalanced teeter-totter, they are also not rhythmically working anymore. They cannot ignore their fatigue, bitterness, or indifference any longer. Both individuals must acknowledge the relationship is not working, so repair can begin. This is the primary step to advocate the possibility of change and growth. We want to get back to an aware and conscious rhythmic dance of the teeter-totter. And this can only happen through growing in personal awareness, taking ownership of the actions and attitudes which have caused damage, and finally, changing hurtful behaviors.

Self-awareness and self-responsibility are the keys to being in a loving and mutually satisfying relationship. They allow us to handle the ambiguity and at times indifference of a relationship. It restrains the impulse to run from a relationship, allowing instead the grace to journey and see if healthy change can occur.

ATTACHMENTS

Unhealthy and dysfunctional relationships in adulthood have their origin in attachments in childhood, according to Bowlby's attachment theory. In 1956, Dr. John Bowlby, a psychoanalyst, began his extensive work on the mother-and-child relationship.[4] He was attempting to understand the distress an infant feels when separated from his mother. There is a stress response a child shows at the time of separation, and these responses demonstrate a correlation with anxious behavior.

For example, if a caregiver is near, attentive, and appropriately responsive to a child—the child will feel secure, loved, and confident. The results are a more playful, smiling, and social child. On the other hand, if a caregiver is inaccessible, inattentive, or inappropriately responds to the child's needs—the child will demonstrate clingy, highly emotional, or anxious behavior. All these actions are attempts to prevent the parent-child separation. The infant will innately act out to overt the loss of support, protection, and care he needs and craves.

Bowlby extended his theory from the parent-child bonding to include caregiver-child, and then eventually to include all human relationships that have an emotional bond between one person and another. He believed that the success of all relationships later in life is dependent on the success of the early primary relationship with a parent or caregiver.

Many adult relationship issues and problems reside in attachment patterns established earlier in life. Not being aware of our unhealthy and unaware subconscious style of attachment precedes much of the pain and problems in relationships later in life. I believe our attachment style from childhood is one of the biggest determining factors in the satisfaction we experience in our present day relationships. When we are not aware of the subconscious attachment, our relationships continue the neglectful, abusive, or anxious style of relating we experienced as a child. And there is nothing messier and out of control than insecure and hurtful primary adult relationships.

Researchers Hazan and Shaver (1987) explored attachments in adulthood, primarily romantic relationships and found that a similar system of behavior occurred between adult romantic partners as between infants and caregivers. They observed the adult romantic relationship and the child-caregiver share the following features:

- Both feel safe when the other is nearby and responsive.
- Both engage in close, intimate, physical contact.
- Both feel insecure when the other is inaccessible.
- Both share discoveries with one another.
- Both play with each other's facial features and exhibit a mutual fascination and preoccupation with each other
- Both engage in "baby talk."[5]

Attachment styles in adulthood are the motivational system working in partner choice, parenting, and behavior patterns in close relationships. Attachments are the particular method or style in which we relate to other people. Our attachment style is primarily established in childhood, during the first two years of life, and vacillates little in adulthood.

Being self-aware and knowing our attachment style helps us to understand both our emotional limits as an adult and highlights the areas that might need some healing and repair.

The subconscious styles subconsciously direct how we behave and relate to close relationships and how we will parent our children. Being self-aware and knowing our attachment style helps us to understand both our emotional limits as an adult and highlights the areas that might need some healing and repair. Below are four styles of attachments - each style has their unique cluster of personality traits and behaviors. Which category do you recognize is most similar to your style?

- **Dismissive-Avoidant Attachment Personality**

The dismissive-avoidant personality is seen in adults who tend to be loners; they don't have a high regard or need for relationships or emotions. They perceive relationships and feelings as less important. They prefer the arena of logic and reality. People who portray the dismissive-avoidant personality deny the need for close relationships, preferring to be highly independent and unaffected by the emotions of a close relationship.

They make their decisions based on what makes sense, objective data, and rational consideration. What is appropriate and correct is more important than how it makes them or others feel. But, for them, choices that make financial, social, and legal sense are more important than how they feel. They prefer to avoid conflict as it stirs too much emotion. They will distance or go to their "cave" instead of engage in situations that involve too much emotion or stress.

Not unexpectedly, those with dismissive-avoidant attachment personality style desire little intimacy in their most significant relationships. The go-to defense mechanism when they perceive the possibility of rejection is to distance themselves from the source of the rejection (that is, their significant other).

In childhood, if the primary caregiver is emotionally unavailable and, as a consequence, uncaring and unaware of the needs of the child, then the child's emotional and sometimes physical needs are frequently not meet, allowing the child to believe that his needs are not important—due to the ineffective influence of the caregiver. The children develop into "little men" and "little women" who take care of themselves. They learn to go inward and isolate. They emotionally remove themselves from feelings and connections with others. They become self-sufficient and don't need anything from anyone.

- **Anxious-Preoccupied Attachment Personality**

People with this style of attachment crave intimacy and a lot of it. They want approval, reassurance, and become overly dependent on how their partner responds to these needs. They believe they have a deeper way of connecting with others and wonder why others are reluctant to get as intimate as they would like them to be.

People who have this insecure, anxious-preoccupied attachment style have low self-regard and self-esteem. They only feel confident when they are in contact with their significant other. Those who exhibit this attachment personality style in adulthood are often over-consumed with a connection, demonstrate high levels of emotional expressing, and tend to be impulsive in their relationships.

Self-critical and insecure are the primary traits of this attachment personality style. Always seeking approval and reassurance from others, they are in a constant state of unrest. The reassurance – which never is enough - continues their self-doubt. Worry and doubt encompass their relationships. The subconscious fear of rejection drives them to be clingy and excessively dependent on their significant relationship.

Inconsistency is the root of insecurity for the anxious-preoccupied personality attachment. In childhood, the parent is inconsistent in tuning into the child's needs. At times, the caregiver is nurturing and appropriate, but at other times harsh and non-caring. Children parented in this manner often become confused and insecure, not knowing what response they will receive. These children are distrusting and will act clingy and anxious to prevent separation.

The unpredictable parent confuses the child and embeds insecurity into the child. These children will not explore much in unfamiliar situations, not want to take a risk, and are leery of strangers—even when the parent is there. They often feel suspicious and distrustful of their parent, but at the same time, they act clingy and desperate. Strangely enough, when the parent leaves the child's sight, the child will cry and shows signs of distress, but when the parent returns, the child is ambivalent.

- **Fearful-Avoidant Attachment Personality**

The fearful-avoidant attachment personality style (sometimes called disorganized attachment) develops when a child grows up in an abusive home. As children, these individuals learn to disconnect from their feelings during times of trauma. As adults, this pattern of detaching from themselves and others continues.

In relationships, all is well until emotional closeness brings repressed fears from the past. They experience the past in the present but are unaware of the source hidden in childhood. They are reliving trauma long forgotten. At this point, feelings repressed in childhood begin to resurface and, with no awareness of them being rooted from the past, they are expressed with full force in the present. The person is no longer in their life today, but the adult is suddenly reliving an old trauma.

Often children and adolescents who have suffered the loss of a significant loved one or experienced sexual and physical abuse demonstrate this attachment personality. They are often insecure, emotionally unaware, and desperate in their relationships. Thus, it sets the stage for an inability to establish and maintain healthy, stable, and close relationships.

Children are caught in a terrible dilemma when abuse occurs—not only from the frightening behavior and possibly life-threatening injury but also by their instinctual response to flee to safety. The person who the child naturally would go to for safety is the one inflicting the harm. The actual source of the child's distress is the caregiver. The child responds by detaching from herself and at times dissociating. She goes to a different place in her mind, a safe place, to push what is happening in the real world far away from awareness.

- **Secure Attachment Personality**

A secure attachment personality is just what it says it is. The person with this personality is secure, confident, and possesses a healthy self-esteem. Adults who have formed secure attachments to caregivers in childhood continue to have secure attachment behavior in adulthood.

They are self-aware and have a healthy sense of self, but yet desire to have close relationships with others. They are differentiated and can handle individuation while they enjoy the intimacy of relationships. They have a strong sense of themselves, and they desire close associations with others. Being able to be both independent and connected, they regard themselves and their relationships in a realistic and positive manner.

Secure attachment personality in adulthood comes from a healthy, emotionally attached caregiver who was sensitive and attuned to the individuals when they were infants through two years of age. The caregiver was consistent and nurturing. In toddlerhood, children begin to be able to use their caregiver as a base from which they can take a risk and explore their world. They become more and more independent, but there is still a healthy connection to their primary caregiver.[6]

In summary, the first three attachment personality styles can cause havoc and loneliness in adult relationships. If we identified ourself in one of the first three styles—don't worry, we are not destined to stay in damaged or unfulfilling relationships. We can intentionally grow and heal; we can become aware by working with a therapist or coach.

One more interesting detail about attachment—we usually choose a partner who has a similar level of function or dysfunction in their attachment style. After reading this section, you might recognize your need for healing, awareness work, or getting help from a professional. I hope you see how imperative raising your self-awareness, through intentional methods (journaling, coaching, counseling, meditation, prayer, etc.), is to reduce the messy choices that can happen in relationships. Positive, interactive relationships based on a healthy, strong interconnectedness will help both partners grow and become better individuals.

TAKING STOCK

Part of the process of becoming more aware and intentional is finding and acknowledging areas where we might be stuck. What area or areas have held you captive from growth and risking being true to yourself? How do you grieve the pain of what has occurred in your life or what you hoped for but never has come to pass? Taking stock of your life is vital for bringing it into focus and beginning to live intentionally.

Take a moment and think about the losses that come to your mind. Your losses may include—but not be limited to—times of losing a loved one by death or betrayal, loss of a job or your health, or loss of your dreams. Identify any area that keeps you from being real in your life and your relationships. Let each incident enter your heart, and see how it feels. These areas you have identified will require some work, but the beginning of the journey is simply recognizing them.

DISCOVERY QUESTIONS: LOSSES

Recommendation: Do Exercise III - CHECKLIST FOR PERSONAL VALUES in Self-Awareness Exercises.

1. What does it mean to you to say, "Loss can be the beginning of a journey?"

    i. Have you experienced this statement to be true in your life? When?

2. Why does author Judith Viorst state that wisdom comes with realizing what we must give up, willingly or unwillingly, in order to grow?

3. If change is such a vital part of life, why is it so difficult to embrace at times?

    i. What change are you avoiding in your life right now?

4. What does "sitting with the unknown" mean to you?

    i. Have you ever had to do this? What was it like?

5. Have you become aware of an area in your life where you need more self-awareness? What area? Is there a change you would like to make that might mean you have to lose something—a reputation, a facade, a relationship, a job—to gain something you desire?

6. What attachment style did you personally identify with the most? Are there any changes, in regard to your attachment style, you would like to make? What are they?

CHAPTER 4
BETRAYAL

Kristen entered my office. I immediately noticed the immense sadness in her eyes. Despite the refined presence and cool demeanor that surrounded her as she entered the room, her eyes told a different story. She decided to try therapy mostly because her sister was persuading her to do so. Although Kristen didn't see any major concerns when she analyzed her life, she finally gave in to her sister's persistence.

In our first session, she told me how life had recently brought much loss—her husband and son had died in a car wreck two years ago, her mother passed away due to cancer a year and a half ago, and now she was in jeopardy of losing her job and the support of dear friends due to rumors and allegations. Kristen noted that even things she once enjoyed couldn't keep her interest. Her eyes dulled, and her body slumped as she started to share her struggles and tell how her heart had lost hope.

"I never thought I would be at this place in life. I never knew how much it could hurt to be living," she began. I asked Kristen if she was at the point of hopelessness where the thought of hurting herself came to mind. She said, "I just don't feel alive. I didn't know how much it could hurt to be alive. I don't want to kill myself, but I do have fantasies of just going away… going far away." I could see her desperation and indifference. I knew she was in the midst of grief. I knew she felt betrayed, betrayed by life itself.

She had hoped and dreamed of a very different life, but now all she felt was disillusioned and grief. Grief, if processed well, does have an endpoint—but grief that is ignored will manifest itself in hopelessness and a chronic feeling of emptiness.

I suspected these losses had fully disillusioned Kristen. She never thought it would be as difficult as it was at this point. Before life had proceeded as was expected, with the occasional bump in the road. It had been pleasant and easy to maneuver. She had never encountered overwhelming hardship, especially such a trial as she was facing now. Few experience the loss she was experiencing in such a short time, but it was harder for someone like Kristen, who had not learned any healthy survival techniques, to embrace and endure hardships. Some people are better prepared to survive the bitter seasons of life. But it is true that *life* happens to everyone. It is part of being human.

Kristen was experiencing denial growing wild in her life. She felt her security crumble beneath her feet while her self-contempt grew stronger, yet she pretended all was well. She found her friends and others that had supported her in the past were also quickly fading. The betrayal and hurt were deteriorating her longings. The essence of who she thought she was became lost in the mire of sorrow. My heart felt much compassion for her, yet all I could offer was a safe place to share the thoughts that she kept safely tucked away. I listened.

Gradually the empathy she received offered her a place to rest. And when the time was right, after some encouragement and coaching, it would be up to her to embrace a new start to life with the awareness of her desires, pain, and disappointments. Kristen would either be free to be true to herself or choose the alternative… settling back into denial and pleasing others for the sake of not feeling abandoned. She would ultimately come to her crossroads and have to choose.

DISILLUSIONMENT

Disillusionment occurs when pain comes and surprises us with sorrow. Webster defines disillusionment as "a feeling that arises from the discovery that something is not what it was anticipated to be, commonly held to be stronger than disappointment, especially when a belief central to one's identity is shown to be false."[1]

Recently, I was taken back to a time in my life when I experienced disillusionment. I was talking with a friend who asked if I would ever go back to my first love. Her question brought me back to a memory ripe with feeling. The feelings weren't as intense as when I had first experienced them, but they were there and easy to access—almost too easy to access, I thought.

Disillusionment occurs when pain comes and surprises us with sorrow.

Emotions flooded in as I quickly went to the memory of the day my fiancé broke our engagement. The invitations were out, flights booked, the dress bought, and, most importantly, I was in love. I remembered his voice over the phone. He sounded so familiar yet so much like a stranger at the same time. His words froze my heart. I thought *It must be a joke*. I asked if it was, but he continued. So many questions entered my mind, but all I could ask was "*Why?*"

Response cards were coming in, and here I was, listening to words that were destroying not only my wedding but my life, from a man I had trusted. I felt rejection, abandonment, but mostly confusion. Things had been fine, or so I thought. We had glitches, like any relationship, but I had known him for ten years, dated him for eight, and now he was choosing to leave me. My heart broke in shock.

I thought for a moment that maybe he had the normal cold feet, but I knew him well enough to know that once he made up his mind, he never changed it. There was nothing more to say. I hung up the phone. I sat alone, knowing none of the answers to the questions that drowned me. Nothing was real. My body was numb. My mind was a fog. The love of my life was leaving, and I couldn't do anything.

Trusting had not been easy for me, especially trusting a man. I had chosen to trust *this* man. I don't know if he reciprocated that gift. I felt so much sadness for what could have been. I had chosen to trust and could not change that decision.

When I went to bed that night, the aloneness was real, but I still had hope that it was all a nightmare and, with the brilliant morning sun, all would be well. I waited for the sun, but it never appeared. Not that day and not the next. I had believed all the lies—his love of me, his devotion to me, our dreams together of children and a fun, romantic marriage. All these lies I had believed hit me with such force. Arrangements needed to be canceled, gifts returned, guests notified, but I was paralyzed. Friends and family were there to do these things, but they couldn't help me live and trust again. I knew that part was up to me.

So when my friend asked the question about my first love, feelings of betrayal reappeared with a vengeance. I felt my heart break again as I remembered the call and his voice saying, "Nancy, we have to talk." I remembered him saying, "It's over." He didn't want to marry me.

I remembered the shock even though it was well over a decade since I had felt it. And I also remembered that all I could do was call a friend and say, "Ann, come get me. Please."

Becoming seized or hijacked by emotion is what Daniel Goleman labels *the hijacking of the amygdala*.[2] The thalamus in the brain is like any skilled air traffic controller; it can quickly react to a potential threat. When it senses danger, it bypasses the cortex—the thinking brain—and the signal goes straight to the amygdala. The amygdala can only react based on previously stored patterns. It is the brain specialist when it comes to emotional matters.

A simple question brought me back to paralyzing disappointment, and it was if that moment was again the moment in which it all happened. Memories of trauma and loss get stored in our brain, ready to be activated by some type of trigger. If these triggers occur frequently, the longings for fulfillment and meaning diminish, and life becomes fragmented. With each hurtful incident—real or imagined—life becomes less fulfilling, less enjoyable. After living like this for a while, we become just crumbs of what we used to be—pieces, fragments of our lives.

Have you ever discovered something was not as good as you believed it to be? Maybe you were excited about a vacation, a relationship, a job, or even a new restaurant, but when you got there, you realized that whatever it was didn't meet your expectations. Disillusionment comes from things even bigger. It happens when you take notice of your life and see it's not what you had hoped it would be.

HOPELESSNESS

Disillusionment can lead to hopelessness, especially if we continually dwell on a loss and do not move on. Hopelessness is deadly to our heart. Without hope there is only mere survival. Research has shown that hopelessness is critically damaging to belief in ourselves, others, and life. When we lose hope, the darker side of life begins to unravel the goodness of life—or at least the hope of that goodness—leaving us with the feeling that life is not worth living.[3]

Such was the case for Mandy. Mandy was in therapy for a substantial amount of time. She was a customer to change, but her journey was long. Her work in her painstaking therapy was deep, and every gain she experienced took tremendous courageous. I respected her with every session as each one unfolded memories of childhood sexual abuse. Her time in therapy marked by moments of sacrifice and a painstaking path of discovering truth. At times, her soul washed in grief as she became brutally aware of her mother's betrayal. Mandy's story began when she was four years old; living with her mom and the numerous men she was told to call "stepdad." I asked Mandy to write a letter to her mother about the betrayal she felt from both her mother and her perpetrators. This is what she wrote:

> *I've rationalized every situation at one point or another in my life. I've rationalized every decision that you did or didn't make to protect me all of the different times in my childhood when no one was there. Today, I sit writing this letter as an adult who still doesn't quite understand how other adults could see what was being done and turn their heads as if nothing was happening. I ask all the "normal" questions. Why? Could they just not see? Were they ignorant? Or did they just not care? My mind can't wrap itself around seeing innocence torn from a child and doing nothing about it. Some of you tried, but when it didn't go as planned, you walked away as if nothing had been said or done. Could you not see in my eyes the pain that I was going through? The emptiness and lack of innocence that must have been there?*
>
> *I am an adult. I am a survivor. I have fought my way back to sometimes feeling like a real person, a person with some value in this world, no matter how little. I am trying to forgive you for betraying me, for looking the other way, for*

not caring. *I'm working hard to do this, but it will never cease to baffle my mind how standing idly by could seem like an option you would want to choose. Through the different trials and difficulties, I have found a great strength—strength I can call my own. While I don't wash my hands of you, I do shake off my sandals and walk on.*

Mandy's hurt was still tangible in her words, but she was no longer the victim. She was validated. Mandy was freeing herself from the chains of her past and the damage from the betrayal. She was finding the hope she needed to live a better life.

When we believe we don't have the power to change our life for the good, we experience hopelessness. Often this occurs with a continual string of loss, betrayal, and disappointments. Shame can also breed hopelessness. After the sexual abuse, Mandy wanted to shrink into a hole and never come out again. Life was far too scary and unpredictable. Mandy chose to stay asleep and not feel all the pain inside. How could she? It was far too much. Choosing to remain asleep, she also couldn't experience hope, pleasure, joy, or peace. To stay asleep was to not feel the pain, even though she missed many good experiences as well.

Then one day she allowed hope to enter her heart and made the choice to wrestle with the pain that was bubbling inside, ready to boil over. She knew somewhere deep inside herself if she chose to grapple with it, healing would happen, and she would find her true life again.

MEMORY FOAM

We often choose familiarity over change and settle into what I call "emotional memory foam." Memory foam is material in a pillow or bed that holds an imprint of our body. We fit nicely into its shape when we lie back in it. It's comfortable, and we know it. Memory foam may work wonderfully for a good night's sleep—but in the journey for an intentional life, it does not serve us well. Choosing what is known versus what is unknown can keep us stuck—never risking the possible uneasiness of facing truth, encountering conflict, or even embracing disappointment from people in our life. Many people fall directly back into memory foam in life situations (careers, finances, relationships, etc.) to keep themselves protected and to feel some sense of control. Its draw is powerful. Even with a purposeful decision to never go back into what has been hurtful or lifeless, we can be overthrown by what feels comfortable. Somehow the cycle continues.

> *Memory foam may work wonderfully for a good night's sleep—but in the journey for an intentional life, it does not serve us well.*

Kristen, my client I mentioned earlier, could have pretended she was the same person as before she encountered such a season of loss. But in doing so, she would have settled for a compartmentalized heart with little boxes to keep her life controlled and protected. She could have settled into the familiar at the cost of losing the ability to fully feel alive. She could have chosen to not let her sorrows break her heart and allow her true-self to emerge from the broken pieces. But Kristen knew she couldn't just survive. Something inside of her wanted more. She wanted to learn how to be honest so that she could heal and living again. Memory foam wasn't going to keep her captive. Kristen allowed herself to fully experience the feeling of grief, letting it roll over her like an ocean wave.

As the author and poet Oriah Mountain Dreamer states, "If we are strong enough to be weak enough, we are given a wound that never heals. It is the gift that keeps the heart open."[4] When we do not allow our hearts to break, we sacrifice our true selves and our true connection with other human beings. Memory foam can either take on an emotionally unavailable or an emotionally dependent persona. The emotionally unavailable person is never really connected, choosing to stay protected and aloof from emotions and true connection. The emotionally dependent person is clinging and overly needy in relationships. Emotional dependency occurs when one believes they cannot survive or be happy without the presence and support of a particular person or group of people. The nurturing or attention from the emotionally dependent person is wonderful at first, but with time the emotionally dependent relationship feels more like bondage or prison. Resentment in these types of relationships will grow as the expectations and demands increase. Yet the need for this person is like memory foam; to risk losing the known comfort of the relationship arouses great anxiety. Unhealthy relationship dependencies are painful to break. The emotional security and intimacy of the relationship is intense, but never free or healthy. The relationship shows signs of unhealthy dependency when either party shows any of the following behaviors:

- Experiences frequent jealousy and possessiveness

- Prefers to spend most of their time alone with this one person and becomes frustrated when it doesn't happen

- Becomes angry or depressed when the other person withdraws from the relationship

- Withdrawals from other relationships

- Takes on the other person's personality, interests, and clothing style

Choosing to walk away from emotionally unavailable and/or emotionally dependent relationships takes courage. It demands a decision to change our fear-based thinking to a more secure and confident thought process. This begins by believing we are enough, we can endure being alone, and we are loved.

RISK OF BETRAYING OUR HEART

Honoring our heart means being honest with ourself and risking the disappointment of others. The ultimate betrayal to our heart and longings is to exist without hope. To live unaware and asleep—never dreaming of our life being more than it is right now. I see my clients, as I myself have done at times, try to avoid hurt by pretending not to have expectations. We think: *It didn't matter if I ever got my promotion,* or, *I didn't really care that I got stood up,* or, *It doesn't matter I wasn't invited to my friend's party.*

Sabotaging is a deliberate action (yet often subconscious) to weaken ourself through subversion, obstruction, disruption, and/or destruction.[5] When we are afraid of having good in our life because of the greater fear of having it ripped from our grasp, we choose to live life in the mundane. And we sometimes actually do subversive things to never experience intimacy, success, hope, etc. At least life is predictable this way. But it is also very confining when we live only in its predictability. It's choosing to stay in a barn that's safe rather than exploring the acres of beauty and adventure outside. We choose the lesser, disrupting any opportunity for fulfillment, so we don't have to risk and really live. But when we push away hope, we push away life as well.

Likewise, when we limit our dreams by consistently asking "what if…"—we paralyze our lives. As Emerson so eloquently pens,

> *Some of your hurt you have cured*
> *and the sharpest you still have survived*
> *But what torment of grief you endured*
> *from evil that never arrived.*[6]

The "what ifs" come in many different thoughts. *What if I get married and he or she cheats on me? What if I do go on this trip and don't have a good time? What if I make the wrong choice about changing jobs and end up hating it?* We can "what if" our life away and never take the risk to really live. To come face to face with our fear and "what-ifs" is to begin to live. But we have to choose to risk and to recognize the pattern. Then do something different. This may mean changing jobs, ending relationships, or simply being more honest in our thoughts and feelings. Choosing today to start taking risks might begin with just a little bit of hope.

It will start with getting to know yourself, the true you, again and discovering what you like, what you want in life, and what you don't. Sometimes the initial step in the self-awareness journey is choosing to have hope in a more fulfilling life by discovering who you truly are.

DISCOVERY QUESTIONS: BETRAYAL

Recommendation: Do Exercise IV - FINDING CORE VALUES in Self-Awareness Exercises.

1. What does *Betrayal* mean to you?

2. Have you ever experienced someone's betrayal? When? What emotions did you experience after you became aware of the betrayal?

3. Give an example of *Memory Foam* in your life? Are there area(s) in your life you are not changing simply because they are familiar and known?

4. Are your ready for change? What the area of your life would like to start the self-awareness journey?

5. How can hope help you make these changes?

PART TWO

THE FOUR PILLARS OF THE *AWARE* LIFE

CHAPTER 5
OPTIMISM

Optimism affects our lives with either its abundance or its lack. I often say that you can tell much about a person through their eyes—their story, their pain, their hope. Even in a photograph, the eyes cannot lie. They tell the truth whether they are dim with despondency or bright with expectancy. Optimism is the key to living life intentionally and genuinely connecting with others. With optimism comes hope; with hope we are able to possess the belief that there will be a positive outcome regardless of life's circumstances. It exists to offer assurance that there is a way for a positive outcome even when there is evidence to the contrary.

Though optimism and hope are closely related they do differ. Optimism is the channel for hope. It is the intentional and deliberate attitude of optimism which is manifests into the emotional state of hope. Both hope and optimism can be fostered to produce positive movements in all of culture. In his book *Principle of Hope* (1986), the German philosopher Ernst Bloch cites utopian projects not only in the social and political realms of well-known theorists (Marx, Hegel, Lenin) but also in architecture, geography, and in multiple works of art (opera, literature, music, dance, film). For Bloch, hope permeates everyday life and is still a strong presence in today's culture.[1] All positive humanistic movements are rooted in the emotional energy of hope.

My client Kristen had experienced much loss in a short time. But the cool demeanor she presented on her first session warmed to a soft, vulnerable presence in the months that followed. Her eyes still told the story of sadness and loss, but after a while, there was a tiny spark of something new. It was hope. She no longer could turn a cold shoulder to her emotions, although the pain was great. She was beginning to feel, and, as a result, beginning to feel alive again. Kristen told me, "It feels like my heart has been in a freezer and is now thawing, and that makes it hurt even more. But one thing I know that I didn't before is that somehow, someway it's going to be okay again."

An intentional life is established in optimism. It is the optimism that allows us to be truthful about who we are and the primary key component that allows the others—humility, forgiveness, and gratitude—to exist. Optimism is the core which fosters hopefulness. It is the the ability to believe life can be good and satisfying. Yet, what if one doesn't have this attitude and is more bent towards the pessimistic—or as some would say—the realistic point of view?

> *Don't cry because it's over, smile because it happened.*
> *~ Dr. Seuss ~*

CHOOSING OPTIMISM

Just like Kristen, any person can be pessimistic and fall into hopelessness. Pessimism often leads to a path of indifference and depression. And as anyone who has suffered from this disabling disorder can testify, it can feel like a dark hole from which there is no escape.

During therapy and coaching sessions with those who struggle in this area, I have seen how certain patterns of thinking seem to fuel depression and move them away from positive thinking. The two that surface most are pessimism and self-loathing. Self-loathing is a pattern of thinking we are a failure, unworthy, and unlovable. Many times professional counseling is needed if the symptoms of depression are severe and/or thoughts of suicide are present. Antidepressant medication may be necessary at times.

In cases not as severe, coaching is an alternative. Counseling focuses on providing information about depression and treatment options, facilitating grieving unresolved losses, healing past emotional traumas, changing unhealthy thinking patterns, and encouraging alternative ways of coping. Where coaching focuses more on replacing unhealthy thoughts with healthier ways to think about self, others, and life; changing unhelpful patterns of thinking; and teaching coping skills. Interestingly, research has shown that successful counseling/coaching can help correct chemical imbalances in the brain as much as antidepressant medications do, only more gradually. All professional treatment is primarily geared to increase hope. If we need a jump-start, it may be best to consider professional help to get the journey started.

What can we do to live a more hopeful life on we own? Living a life that is true to who we are can give a certain amount of energy to see life through a different, more optimistic lens. I have found that the people who naturally exude optimism have certain key components of hope embedded in them. Why do some people radiate hope and joy and others do not? Those who are optimistic may be genetically and/or environmentally prone toward hopefulness and joy; they have a natural upbeat and positive personality, or they may have learned it from positive and cheerful parent, or they may have worked very hard to learn and live a life of hope. If we had the chance to experience life in their shoes—to experience a better life, more satisfying relationships, and a successful career—wouldn't we want more of the good stuff that encourages such positive results? The key components to instilling optimism are listed below. Read through them and see where you are strong and which ones may need some work.

KEY COMPONENTS OF INSTILLING OPTIMISM

ATTITUDE

Attitudes and thoughts can be developed by an outside source, such as family, media, and community. These thoughts develop into images (or ideas) in our conscious mind. We then impress the images upon our subconscious mind. This produces feelings that can cause us to behave in a particular manner whether that approach is positive or negative. In turn, these attitudes produce behaviors that either have good, healthy effects or damaging ones.

One of my clients, Sara, had been severely traumatized by sexual abuse and abandonment in her childhood. She had learned that if she expected very little to nothing out of life, she would never be disappointed. It was working, she thought, until she met Jim—the man she wanted to marry. Sara realized she had to fully let him into her heart. The defensive patterns she learned as a child were blocking not only the harmful experiences of life but also the pleasant experiences of connection, love, and gratitude. Sara told me as she sat in my office, "I am terrified of life." And I could see she was. She wouldn't risk in love or in life. She made sure she was always in control and had an exit door. But then she found a loving spiritual relationship with God, and a man who was good and who loved her. And for Sara to embrace that goodness, her attitude toward life had to change.

> *"When we see choice instead of chance, we
> become the creator of our experience."*

Can attitudes be changed? The only way to improve the consequences of our life is to first identify our outlook. Are we more pessimistic or optimistic? Do we generally see life with a positive lens full of hope and possibilities or a negative lens of gloom and mistrust? Sara needed to identify through which lens she was seeing her life and then acknowledge the fear that kept her stuck. She knew she was responsible for how she perceived and lived the rest of her life. Sara had to dig deep to muster up enough hope to believe her life could be different. She had to choose to be a victim no longer. Just like Alan Cohen stated in *Joy is my Compass*, "When we see choice instead of chance, we become the creator of our experience."[2]

The glass-half-empty mentality (pessimism) has been observed to come from rigid thinking that has been learned from significant influences in a child's life. Dr. Martin Seligman, a past president of the American Psychological Association, has researched how our thinking becomes ingrained either into the negative or into the positive. In his recent research, Dr. Seligman indicates that depression is on the rise, signifying that a negative rigid pattern of thinking is evolving. He found that depression is ten times more common now than it was two generations ago. Why such a drastic change? Two of the contributing factors Dr. Seligman discusses are listed below:

1. *I-We Balance*: We have become rampantly individualistic and more isolated physically and emotionally from others, as opposed to our grandparents—who had larger connections with family, friends, and community.

2. *Victimology*. Victimology, in its simplest form, is the study of the victim or victims of a particular offender. Victim

thinking is on the rise. It's the feeling of being powerless and not having the ability to change our life. This type of thinking is the foundation of hopelessness. It has been seen that some people are prone to be victims due to race, sex, past victimization, and attitude of powerlessness. When we choose to stay in the victim role, there is a nullifying of the need for change and responsibility. We become void of the power to take full accountability for our lives. The major cost of victim thinking is the attrition of responsibility, which is paralleled to lower self-esteem.[3]

In contrast to hopelessness and victim thinking, there has been an increased interest in the benefits of optimism. What makes someone an optimist? When a hindrance or negative event occurs, the optimistic individual has three characteristics that are prominent in his or her thinking:

1.) The event is seen as temporary rather than permanent.

2.) The event is viewed as local and not global.

3.) The individual is able to see contributing circumstances versus internal blame for the event.

Research shows people who sustain an optimistic view have less depression, have more career success, have better physical health, and have better interpersonal relationships.[4]

RESILIENCY

Resiliency is a definite characteristic of optimism. Resilience is ability to bounce back from a negative life event—such as the loss of a loved one, health issues, a poor job review, or relationship problems. It's the capability to keep going, finding the lemon in the lemonade.

Resiliency produces a quality of depth in a person. We know these people. They usually have an unrecognizable attraction to them. They exude peace and confidence that make others want to hang out with them. Deep down, they know all issues and problems take time—there are no quick fixes. Thus, they are able to stay present and rest in the moment, believing that all will be well in time.

To see life as a process is to see the continuation of events and seasons that make up the whole of life. To stay optimistic is the ability to endure a difficult season, knowing that it is only part of life's journey. There will be periods of happiness, seasons of tears, and seasons of growth—and they all must enter into the mix of life. One hard season—like a cold winter—will give way to a new one, with all the possibilities of spring.

SAFETY

Safety is often found in the most unexpected places. Often safety breeds a newness, a sense of hope and optimism. Brokenness allows new growth in people's lives. It is usually in the understanding and unconditional love of a dear friend, a spouse, a parent, or even a coach or counselor. People can bring such incredible harm, but they can also bring healing. We all need a place that is safe enough to reveal our humanity.

Emotional safety is often the bridge from hopelessness to hopefulness. To be safe is to experience the complete comfort of knowing that we are in the presence of a person or people who know us well and have seen our strengths and our struggles. They have seen us at our best and at our worst; they have known us and accepted us when no one else would. They are safe; they are the people who will instill hope in us again. This desire for healing connection is eloquently penned in the following quote:

> I want to live in intimacy and being known even when time together is brief. When we meet, I don't want to ask you what you do for a living. I want to know what you ache for when that door of longing swings open and if you have the courage to feel your own desire. Tell me something you have not told yourself for a very long time. Let it come up from your belly, so we can be surprised together. We will sit here, together, for as long as it takes, waiting for it to come. It's hard to wait alone. There have been moments when I was afraid my longing would never find me again. All my journeys have been in search of desires I have abandoned.[5]

EMBRACE CHANGE

At times achieving our passions and our highest goal involves closing one door to someone or something to make room for something new, different and good. Though the horizon may be dark, hope rises when opportunity is recognized. The ability to choose change or react to loss with optimism is the ultimate goal of moving toward an *aware life*.

We do not need to forget our past journey to have hope for a fulfilled future. To be genuine is to embrace our pain, believing we will still exist—wiser, softer, and kinder. Pain brings everyone to the point of having to make choices—choices that many times require change and growth. Optimism is powerful—it instills the ability to have hope that good will come again. It reminds us we do have choices, all kinds of choices, even when we feel we don't.

DISCOVERY QUESTIONS: **OPTIMISM**

Recommendation: Do Exercise V - QUESTIONS TO ASK YOURSELF in Self-Awareness Exercises.

1. What does *Optimism* mean to you?

2. What area(s) of your life do you have a negative lens? What would change if you had a positive lens in this area(s)?

3. When Alan Cohen states:
    "When we see choice instead of chance, we become the creator of our experience." What do you think he means? Do you live this way?

4. Lack of taking responsibility for your actions actually goes hand in hand with lower self-esteem. Have you seen this to be true?

5. What are the three characteristics of an optimistic individual when something bad happens to them?

   i.

   ii.

   iii.

6. What area of your life do you want to be more optimistic? How can you start that process today?

CHAPTER 6

HUMILITY

Humility, genuine humility, is a rare and precious character. It is not low self-esteem but the ability to allow another the place of honor and to be fully transparent without shame. I believe humility is often misunderstood. Recently I heard a joke that captures how true humility can be tricky to attain.

> Walking into the empty sanctuary of the synagogue, a rabbi was suddenly possessed by a wave of mystical rapture and threw himself onto the ground, proclaiming, "Lord, I'm nothing!"
> Seeing the rabbi in such a state, the cantor felt profoundly moved by similar emotions. He too threw himself down on the ground, proclaiming, "Lord, I'm nothing!"
> Then, way in the back of the synagogue, the janitor also threw himself to the ground, and he too shouted, "Lord, I'm nothing," whereupon the rabbi turned to the cantor and whispered, "Look who thinks he's nothing!"

Even in our attempts to be humble, our hearts often fall so short. It doesn't matter how spiritually attuned we may be or the name we are called—rabbi, priest, pastor. Humility is hard to maintain. Humility is the second key in living the intentional *aware life*. Humility is the characteristic that urges us to go more than halfway to meet the needs and requests of others. It defeats aggression and pride. Rather than "me first," humility says, "no, you first."

Humility distinguishes the wise leader from the arrogant power-seeker. It seeks forgiveness and heals relationships. When we are humble, we value and give dignity to others. Lately humility has been seen as a key to both personal and business success. It is strength not frailty. In the book *Good to Great: Why Some Companies Make the Leap . . . and Others Don't* by Jim Collins, the quality of humility is identified as one of the best indicators for success in the leadership of companies.[1]

It is possible to maintain confidence about who we are—our achievements and worth—and also maintain a sense of humility. Humility is self-confidence. It allows others to be the center of attention, and we accept and acknowledge the work, talents, abilities, and authority of others. Humility brings contentment and an inner peace and is captured in the bold act of admitting that we made a mistake. It is being truthful about our shortcomings—and as we accept our own shortcomings, we are able to accept others' as well.

RELATIONSHIPS AND HUMILITY

Truth and humility are inseparable in regard to intentional living. As the English writer Charles Caleb Colton penned, "The greatest friend of truth is Time, her greatest enemy is Prejudice, and her constant companion is Humility."[2]

> *"The greatest friend of truth is Time, her greatest enemy is Prejudice, and her constant companion is Humility."*

Healthy relationships are founded on becoming transparent, which fosters trust. Greg Baer says in his book *Real Love*,

> We all want that (real love) but few of us are prepared to *be* the kind of truly loving partner that such a relationship requires. Before we can participate in a mutually loving relationship, we must learn to tell the truth about ourselves, feel unconditionally loved, and learn to love others.[3]

Most people, if not all, desire to be good human beings, to bring value and kindness to life. To demonstrate these desirable characteristics, we must first wrestle with the demons of pride. Being humble is also being vulnerable. Vulnerability means "capable of being… wounded."[4] Yet there is strength in being vulnerable. Paradoxically speaking, we become weak to find strength, as Paula Rhinehart captures in the following quote:

> You step into the difficult place and find you are not blown away. Hearing a friend's criticism, you resist being defensive. You take the humble road, and find that it is the means of walking straight and tall. You say the words you need to say. In these kinds of moments, you can almost feel your soul expand.[5]

A DEEPER LOOK

We all have heard of or personally experienced friendships and marriages that dissolve over heated words. With all the damage of anger, resentment, prejudice, and gossip—which are all constructs of pride—it would seem valid to honor humility. But it is a rare commodity.

Even for those of us fortunate enough to have humility and empathy instilled in us early in life, it is still a daily challenge to exhibit. Why was it so important to learn these values when we were children, and why does it continue to be even more essential in adulthood? The answer rests in our ability to care for and intentionally maintain relationships. Humility keeps us from becoming egocentric individuals. To feel others' hurt, their embarrassment, their struggles, is vital for genuine connection. As adults, we often forget the importance of humility and empathy as we relate with one another. Much of this is due to the fast paced world we live in and our tendency towards selfishness and pride. Protection of self is innate in who we are. The ego is a fragile entity that protects itself from hurt and humiliation through pride. Being humble is counter-intuitive to the more self-protective ego. Humility is risky and put the prideful ego on alert. Thus, only with healthy self-awareness and strong self-confidence can humility be present and powerful in our life.

KIND BOUNDARIES

Robert Frost in his poem "Mending Wall" shows a profound illustration of this idea of boundaries. His declaration that "good fences make good neighbors" poetically states that some distance between people produces good relationships.[6] No matter how close a relationship is, healthy differentiation is essential to maintaining growth and fulfillment.

Limits on our time, money, relationships, time and emotions are all contained by our personal boundaries. Boundaries are the imaginary lines telling people how much we will let others in, what we may or may not do for them, and when they cross the lines what they should expect. When we have healthy boundaries, we spend our time and energy wisely. We are real and honest in what we say and do. We don't waste our time or money on relationships or things that are not good for us. We have the power to say no to some and yes to others.

Kind boundaries may seem like an oxymoron, but in self-aware living, they go hand in hand. We choose what is healthy for us and then can be truly authentic in how we interact with others. Boundaries are individual decisions—what we will or won't do, what we like and don't like, and how emotionally close others can be to us. Kind boundaries are like personal boundaries, yet they are carried out in compassion and humility. They foster taking responsibility for their contribution to any unhealthy situation. They invite grace to be the cushion between rigid boundaries—which prevent others from getting near —and the lack of boundaries that allow manipulation. Kind boundaries are flexible, yet firm.

Some people find it hard to disappoint others. Thus, they have difficulty saying no. It is especially difficult for those with caretaking issues, those who feel their primary purpose is to assist others, even if it is to their detriment. Saying no and thereby keeping proper boundaries is difficult when the consequences involve disapproval, especially if it's from someone close. Fear of losing a friend, a partner, a lover, or a co-worker may keep us saying yes to things we don't want to do. And no to the things we do want to do. But each time, we become less genuine to who we are. Whenever we say yes when we want to say no, we let someone (or something) invade our boundaries. Ultimately we are interpreting a request as a demand. We're saying to ourself we have no choice because we can't take the risk of rejection or loss.

However, with kind boundaries, we always have a choice. People trust and respect those who are grounded and clear. If we say no with humility and kindness, respect from others will follow. We will also gain respect for ourself in the process.

Boundaries define who we are and how we live. When we approach situations from a perspective of humility, we become more open-minded. We spend more time in that beautiful space of the beginner's mindset—the brilliant place of willing to learn from what others have to offer. We move away from pushing our point of view to listening, from insecurity to security, from seeking approval to seeking enlightenment. We forget about being perfect, and we enjoy being in the moment. As we remain real in every situation, others are invited to be genuine as well.

> *Boundaries define who we are and how we live.*
> *When we approach situations from a perspective of*
> *humility, we become more open-minded.*

Allison, a beautiful, blonde, forty-year-old woman, had provocative manners that allowed her to get much attention from wealthy men. She could always find a man to take care of her. Allison came to counseling because she was struggling with moodiness and unusual outbursts of anger. She was depressed, feeling empty, and inadequate. Her validation came from outside forces: the men she dated, the clothes she wore, the house she lived in, and the attractiveness of her friends. She was compelled to have only the best, and only those who adored her, by her side. When that failed, which it often did, she felt sad and at times even suicidal—only relieved by her next conquest. Allison was constantly chasing someone or something to make her feel better about herself. She destroyed her own and others' boundaries in her selfish pursuit of happiness.

Allison displayed weak internal boundaries steeped in unhealthy defense mechanisms and pursuits. She was in great need of change.

As she progressed through her counseling session, she became aware of her unhealthy pattern of allowing others to be her source of happiness. She realized she had never set boundaries of what she did and didn't want in her life. She was too afraid to be alone, too afraid to fail. She kept her world safe, but not alive. The irritability and sadness she experienced were symptoms of settling for so much less than what her heart desired.

In therapy, I introduced Alison to the concept of kind boundaries—the ability to make and keep our boundaries while accepting our responsibility of how we have contributed to the dysfunction. Allison grew to understand and live by this concept. With humility, she acknowledged her part of the unhealthy manner in which she had been living and made the needed changes in her life and relationships. Gradually, her life became more genuine and fulfilling. She embraced the knowledge that she was enough; worthy in who she was—just exactly as she was.

THE ART OF HEARING ANOTHER'S HEART

The art of listening is rare. It is an incredible and precious gift to receive. Unfortunately, in today's fast paced society it is uncommon to experience the presence of someone choosing to fully listen to what we are saying - and have the skills to understand what we are trying to express. The goal of listening is not just to hear what the other is saying but to *understand* what they are saying. It is a humble position of being present and earnest with another person, especially when we have a point of view we desperately want to express.

Listening is a careful art that facilitates a connection few other acts can foster. Time seems to fly by when we are engaged in a good conversation. We experience a connection of our soul with someone, which fosters openness and reveals another layer of our heart. Sounds wonderful, doesn't it? Sadly, though, it doesn't happen often enough because our minds are on our own thoughts, our own problems, or we are thinking of the next creative thing to say. Usually, listening is not about the other person; it is still about us. It's not being real and open with someone, which would allow them to be feel understood and accepted. In other words, we are still painting the picture we want instead of allowing another to paint their pictures on our canvas.

Intentional listening is achieved with understanding—when that black-and-white words evolve into something with color and dimension. It's not about who is right or wrong; it's about taking the opportunity to risk understanding another person's heart. Listening means that when someone is speaking, we are *present* and hearing every word.

When we are living intentionally and humbly, listening becomes an opportunity for us to grow and experience the gift of being fully present—and to sincerely learn about—another individual.

PRACTICING HUMILITY

There are times when choosing to be humble is particularly difficult, and any attempt at meekness fails. If we find ourself in such a situation, consider developing a plan to ensure that the circumstances don't lead us to lose our grace. Below are some helpful approaches to handling a difficult situation.

- *Reflect.* Take the time to think and reflect on what would be the best approach. Catch yourself if you blindly slip into preaching or parenting a friend, a co-worker, or a spouse.

- *Seek.* Ask for others' input on how you are doing with listening, and help them see you are trying to understand their point of view. Ask, "How am I doing?" It takes humility to ask such a question and even more humility to consider the answer.

- *Stop.* Learning to listen is essential to being humble. Stop talking and allow the other person to be the focus of attention. There is something very liberating in this strategy. This will help you not just be a genuine teller of the truth but a genuine listener of the truth as well.

- *Speak.* State back what you have heard, and see if what you are hearing is what they are trying to communicate. It is with openness, you demonstrate your sincere desire to hear what is being spoken, allowing real connection and communication to occur.

When we practice humility—the intentional *aware life* is evident. Self-awareness grows, careers bloom, and relationships are repaired.

DISCOVERY QUESTIONS: HUMILITY

Recommendation: Do Exercise VI - INTENTIONAL ACTIONS in Self-Awareness Exercises.

1. Do you believe humility is actually a result of self-confidence? How so?

2. What is an example in your life of a humble boundary?

3. "The goal of listening is not just to hear what the other is saying but to understand what they are saying." What does this mean to you? How do you know the difference when you are being listened to? Or when you are listening to someone else? Why is humility vital to be able to listen in this manner?

4. In what area of your life do you need more humility?

5. How can you practice more humility in your life?

CHAPTER 7
FORGIVENESS

How does forgiveness relate to the intentional *aware life?* There are many interpretations of what genuine forgiveness means. To settle on one definition of forgiveness minimizes its all-encompassing effect, but I will define what I see as true forgiveness of self and others later in this chapter. To be intentional is not to be blinded by bitterness or resentment. It doesn't matter if that resentment is toward another person or towards ourself. Being genuine is accepting that the human journey can be rough. It's a journey in which we all get banged up along the way—if not by others then by our own self-loathing

If we don't journey, the hurt we have experienced or the shame we have come to know so well will keep us a prisoner. We hide the truth of who we are in a safe place that preserves our withered soul. The *aware life* requires realness, truth, and forgiveness. It requires intentionality and sustainability. It beckons us to dig deep and find the open wounds and hurts that continue to wreak havoc in our life then to choose to fully engage in the process of healing.

MEMORIES AFTER A PERSONAL TRAUMA

August 8th was a day like any other—except for the fact that I was taking Beth, my best friend of over twenty years, back to the airport. She had come to visit a few months after I was married.

We had a wonderful visit that was full of laughter, intimate chats, and fun. Beth was returning to Denver to be with her two sons and husband. It was early in the morning, and the sun was starting to rise. The warmth of the day provided a soothing balm. I was saddened that my friend was leaving but delighted with the time we were able to spend together. She and I set off, enjoying our drive to the airport. Then, without warning, there was darkness. I heard the smash of metal but never saw the truck that hit us. Somehow I had not seen the other vehicle as I merged onto the highway, and he missed seeing me. He was traveling fifty-five to sixty-five miles per hour and hit the side of the car exactly where Beth was sitting. There was no light and no sound until I awoke to a feeling of dread, which followed me for years. I didn't know what had happened, but I knew from the earthquake in my stomach it wasn't good. I yelled, "Oh, God, help!" as I looked at my dear friend, whose eyes deviated to the right and who was beginning to have a seizure. Being a nurse, I quickly knew she had brain damage, and I feared the person who hit me was dead. Later, I found my fear was true. I lay there with a concussion, broken ribs and collarbone, but in the midst of the physical pain, it was the emotional pain that I couldn't bear. I cried and prayed, "Help Beth, help the person who hit us, and help me." Then I sank to the ground in the realization of the long and painful process that lay ahead. I just wanted to disappear. In the book Trauma and Recovery: The Aftermath of Violence—from Domestic Abuse to Political Terror, author Judith Herman states: Traumatized people relive the event as though it were continually recurring in the present. They cannot resume the normal course of their lives, for the trauma repeatedly interrupts. Even normally safe environments may come to feel dangerous, for the survivor can never be assured that she will not encounter some reminder of the trauma.[1] I continued to relive the accident for some time, physically and especially emotionally. A year and a half after my car wreck, walking with a friend, I saw some random skid marks on the street. I wasn't thinking about the accident at all; in fact, I was enjoying my day. But upon seeing the marks, I instantly heard the sound of crunching metal. I was haunted by the sounds from the flashback. My heart started to pound quickly, and feelings of fear arose. The marks on the road were the external trigger that instantly brought me back to that horrible day. The flashback caused a hyper-arousal response of my autonomic nervous system, producing a sequel of psychological and physiological responses. Triggers can be external, or they can be internal—such as hunger, sexual arousal, or even an emotional state like sadness. Wherever they arise, triggers carry us directly to the memory of the trauma. These memories elicit psychological states of terror, anxiety, and/or the physiological states of numbness and withdrawal. When triggers occur, the memory of loss or trauma can elicit a sense of hopelessness and powerlessness. Often a feeling of shame accompanies these feelings with thoughts of "I should not have made that decision," "I should have known better," or "I am bad." The alienating effect of shame can interfere with intimacy in many areas: spiritually, sexually and emotionally with an intimate partner, relationally with family and friends, and personally with identity issues. Managing these feeling of loss and shame in a healthy manner can foster an awakening of the soul to change. If the positive aspects of change are not embraced in life, individuals who encounter trauma, loss, betrayal, and disillusionment will believe on some level that they allowed these things to occur—and thus feel powerless to change anything. They see that their efforts in the past have been fruitless, so they conclude all will be fruitless in the future. This lie is powerful and must be exposed if true growth is to occur. After the accident, I struggled immensely with guilt and shame. My best friend was still alive, but she had a head injury that would alter the rest of her life. I was to blame. I had been driving. Why didn't I see the other truck? Why didn't it happen to me instead of her? I had so many questions and very few answers. I had to face the shame, learn to forgive myself, and start to deal with the loss. Beth's healing journey was long, and she has successfully adapted to her new life. But our friendship was changed, and the emotional strain and distance was difficult to accept. My struggle to accept this traumatic experience was one I wrestled with for a long time. I didn't want to admit that my best friend now had a significant brain injury, and I was at fault for driving the car. I didn't want to face that reality. It didn't match up with how I wanted to see myself. It didn't fit. I wanted to see myself as bringing good into others' lives, and the car wreck and its results didn't align with that view. But I was powerless to change it. I had to accept this trauma as part of my friend's life, the other driver's family's life, and my life. I had to immerse myself in the concept of the pain of Beth's brain injury, the loss of my friendship with her, the grief of unintentionally killing someone, and, mostly, my responsibility for all this hurt. I knew if I didn't learn to sit with this reality, I would forever live in guilt—which would keep me stuck in a lifeless ambivalence. I had to intentionally accept this trauma experience as part of my story, and I had to learn to embrace it. I had to.

WHY FORGIVE?

To choose to forgive is not an easy task but a necessary one. The impact of forgiving or not forgiving is lived out in every aspect of our life. Our relationships, health, and fulfillment can all be affected by this choice. Forgiveness is a process that goes unseen and hidden from others' sight; it is an option only visible to our own heart. Yet the results are generalized to your whole life.

Elizabeth Gilbert in her book *Eat, Pray, Love* states forgiveness took on a new shape that brought more truth, which helped free her from shame and sorrow. "If even one broken and limited human being could experience even one such episode of absolute forgiveness and acceptance of her own self, then imagine—just imagine—what God, in all His eternal compassion, can forgive and accept."[2]

Those who choose forgiveness as a lifestyle often experience more career success, fulfilling relationships, and profound peace. They don't let bitterness, pride, or expectancy inhabit or inhibit their lives. It has also been noted those that let forgiveness be a primary character in their life enjoy higher self-esteem due to the ability to maintain close, significant relationships.[3]

WHAT FORGIVENESS IS AND WHAT IT IS NOT

A definition of forgiveness that resonates with me comes from Robert D. Enright and Joanna North in their book *Exploring Forgiveness*. They say,

> When unjustly hurt by another, we forgive when we overcome the resentment toward the offender, not by denying our right to the resentment, but instead by trying to offer the wrongdoer compassion, benevolence, and love; as we give these, we as forgivers realize that the offender does not necessarily have a right to such gifts.[4]

Adopting an open viewpoint of life is vital to living freely. It is important to see what is keeping us stuck and thus blocking our perspective. It is fundamental to obtaining an objective view. A great analogy of an objective view versus subjective view involves using the Grand Canyon as a metaphor for our whole life. There in front of us, in all its grandeur, beauty, and vastness, is the Grand Canyon. Pretend we take a book and bring it up to where it is actually touching our nose. Now look. How much of the Grand Canyon can we see? Not much at all. That's an example of a subjective view. But if we take that very same book and pull it out as far as our arm will extend, how much of the Grand Canyon can we see now? A lot more, right? Think of that book as your issue. In an objective view, the issue is still there, but we can see more of the rest of the view—more of the rest of our life. It gives us more perspective instead of just focusing on the one area that is draining our energy and calling for our attention. Maintaining an objective view of a hurtful situation helps gain perspective of our hurt from a larger perspective. It brings in objectivity, empathy, and self-awareness – maybe for the better because of how we have emotionally grown. Having an objective view allows us to forgive more often, more quickly, and more deeply. It prevents the dysfunctional position of inflexibility and stagnation.

Likewise, looking at the areas where there is a lack of forgiveness in our life broadens our view. A truer, objective view facilitates false assumptions about ourself and others. Forgiveness is removing those assumptions so that beliefs and ways of relating are more congruent to our true-self. There are three choices when it comes to forgiveness: 1) forgiveness refusal, 2) cheap forgiveness, and 3) authentic forgiveness.

FORGIVENESS REFUSAL

In many situations of hurt, the first response—and sometimes the only choice by some—is to choose to refuse forgiveness. The *refusal to forgive* is the most rigid and, frequently, the first response individuals have when they have been hurt. In hopes of revenge and hostility, our true-self is lost. Such a choice can lead to a life of negativity and resentment. The lack of forgiveness demands a staggering toll. It can shape our experience of life and render us emotionally dependent on the person who wronged us.

When we refuse to forgive, we become frozen in time to the incident or incidents that produced such hurt and damage. Time stands still, and yet life goes on without us. Have you met someone who seems fixated on an event that occurred a year, two, ten, or even two decades ago? Life stopped at that time, and the heart has not softened. Refusing to forgive not only cuts us off from others, but it also cuts us off from our own life and happiness. We make the decision to continue to punish the offender. Our freedom and fulfillment lie beyond our reach, inaccessible due to the resentment in which we live. We wonder how we could ever have been so dumb, so fallible to trust someone. We think that from now on we will trust only ourselves. But anger at others only revises our dreams and connections, leaving us alone and wanting.

When we refuse to forgive, we become frozen in time to the incident or incidents that produced such hurt and damage.

Andrew stated on his paperwork that he was thirty years old, but the wrinkles and hard lines on his face told a different story. He came to therapy because his girlfriend gave him an ultimatum. "Go to therapy or I'm done with the relationship." She said she was tired of Andrew's angry outbursts. She never knew when he would "just lose it" and start raging and arguing with her. These events left her shaken and untrusting. She was ready to leave him if he didn't change.

Andrew thought his anger wasn't "that bad" and even thought it was appropriate and healthy. Yet, while obtaining his relationship history, I could see the lines in his face deepen, and his eyes become hard when I asked about his past girlfriends. Feeling I had hit a sensitive place, I pressed in further to learn more. Andrew then told me the story of his last girlfriend. They had dated three years and were planning on getting married. Until the day he found she had been cheating on him with his best friend. Angry and hurt, Andrew told her to leave and never come back. He looked at me and said, "That was a deal breaker, and I will never forgive her." And he hadn't, but unknowingly he kept the anger from his previous girlfriend alive and well in the anger he displayed toward his current girlfriend. I asked him if he wanted to explore how refusing to forgive affected the expression of anger in his current relationships. Andrew quickly stated, "I will never forgive her," and ended his therapy sessions.

Andrew was a man who felt he had the right to never have bad things happen to him. Life doesn't work that way. His anger came from a place of entitlement which didn't foster forgiveness or empathy for others. His previous girlfriend had been hurtful and wrong, but it was Andrew's inability to forgive would continue to bring him pain in his current relationship, until one day, hopefully, he will choose to deal with the hurt and suffering from his ex-girlfriend's and best friend's betrayal.

CHEAP FORGIVENESS

The second choice in forgiveness is *cheap forgiveness*. I love working with people who are bumping up against old wounds and anger, thinking they have already dealt with their issues. Cheap forgiveness is a typical response from those who are trying to convince others or even themselves by saying they have forgiven their offender though they still hold a strong and significant grudge. My job is to break down the façades and bring out the truth even if it's ugly, nasty, and raw. The real self emerges when *shoulds* of life are in their appropriate place, nowhere at all. Sometimes people think it is not acceptable to express anger, frustration, or even hatred towards those that hurt them. They are told they "should" get over it. They "should" move on. Their negative emotions are not allowed and not dealt with appropriately so they can move on in a healthy manner towards forgiveness. Cheap forgiveness gives the illusion of doing the right thing without dealing with the emotional damage. It can also minimize the offense or allow hurt and even abuse to continue. Being in this position is far from living the intentional *aware life*.

> *Cheap forgiveness gives the illusion of doing the*
> *right thing without dealing with the emotional damage.*

A good example of cheap forgiveness comes from a client of mine. Shelly visited my office twice. She had been plagued by depression and surprising explosions of anger. She'd heard that I worked with people with anger issues, so she came in to see me. Our first meeting went well, and she was very sweet—maybe a little too sweet—and she agreed to come back for another session.

In the following session, I was met with a similar version of the person I had seen before, but she was a little gruffer, a little edgier. Still, she smiled and said all was well. When I asked her how she was doing, she acknowledged that she didn't like some issues I had asked during our last session. I thought back and reviewed mentally how it went. The only area I recalled in which she was uncomfortable was when mentioning her past sexual abuse. We hadn't stayed on that subject for long, as I was trying to get a full history of all her struggles. I remembered her telling me, "I have already forgiven him, so it doesn't bother me anymore."

I made a mental note of her comment and thought, *That was a quick response—too quick. Is there more there or not? Guess we'll see where she leads me.* Not saying anything to her, I let it go as she continued her story.

The edginess Shelly displayed during our second session quickly revealed I was stirring a pot that didn't want to be awakened. She said, "What happened with my cousin was a long time ago, and I don't see any need to bring that up." I realized she didn't want to go there, and she wasn't ready. So, I continued on with our session, not returning to this subject. It was her story, and when she was ready—she would tell it.

The cheap forgiveness she had given her cousin was losing its glue. She was trying desperately to avoid the buried emotions that were about to come undone. Shelly had worked through some forgiveness but hadn't processed all the damage that had occurred in her life due to one man's selfish act. She didn't want to see the anger, the depression, the low self-esteem, and sexual frustrations that might have been produced partially, if not entirely, by his actions. And the Band-Aid of cheap forgiveness wasn't holding anymore. What she had lived with for so long could no longer be taken care of quickly. The journey might have been painful, and she didn't want to go there. I honored her choice. It was hers to make. Shelly never came back, or at least she hasn't come back yet. Cheap forgiveness doesn't heal, it doesn't hold, and it will fall apart. The hurt must be grappled with to arrive at authentic forgiveness.

AUTHENTIC FORGIVENESS

Authentic forgiveness is the third and healthiest choice. The decision to fully understand and come to terms with the damage done by an offense is vital for authentic forgiveness. This process recognizes the event or events for what they are. And it does not allow for hiding behind a veneer or minimizing the event. We have to reckon with broken relationships, damaged identities, and hurtful choices made from wounded areas in our lives. We may not want to grieve because it hurts. We may be like Shelly, not wanting to truly process the pain. At times, authentic forgiveness may involve confronting our offender and other times it does not. The process of confrontation can be scary and painful. Its benefits have to outweigh its risks. If not, then I don't advocate confrontation. If confronting the offender is determined to be helpful on the journey of forgiveness; here are two scenarios the confrontation may take:

1) The offender can't or won't engage in the healing process and, because of this, is unwilling (or unable) to make amends for his or her action. Thus, repair or reconciliation is not possible.

2) The offender engages in the healing process to gain forgiveness and works toward possible relationship repair and reconciliation.

When two people enter an intimate dance, held together by an interpersonal violation, the offender must work hard to earn forgiveness through genuine, generous acts of repentance. The hurt party, too, works hard at letting go of any resentment and any desire for retribution. Together they redress the injury and find a way to forgive.[5] Again, forgiveness does not mean forgetting. We cannot forget a hurt, but we *can* decide to let go of the bitterness toward the offender. We can also choose to let go of the bitterness we carry towards the offender and possible towards ourself.

It is too easy to react to life's disappointments with anger. Holding a grudge can consume us and eventually destroy us. Grudges can cloud judgment and lead to acts of revenge that can never be reversed. They can also inhibit the values that foster genuine relationships. The humble, forgiving temperament can settle quarrels and interrupt the damaging effects of pride and self-righteousness. It cannot predict or control others' choices, but it sure can help us sleep better.

So what does authentic forgiveness look like? How can we be confident that we are fully and entirely forgiving the person who has hurt us? Below is a list of the important ingredients for authentic forgiveness:

- Honoring the full span of our emotions.
- Letting go of the need for revenge.
- Continuing to seek an honorable resolution.
- Ceasing to obsess about the injury.
- Protecting ourself from further abuse.
- Having empathy for the offender as we become aware of our own personal struggles.
- Confronting our false assumptions about what happened.
- Deciding what kind of relationship, if any, we want with the one who hurt us.
- Forgiving ourself for our own feelings.
- Re-engaging with life in a full and intentional manner.

SELF-FORGIVENESS

Sometimes the person we need to forgive is not someone else, but it's the one in the mirror. After my car wreck, I had to learn to forgive myself so I could fully live again. This was not an easy experience, and it took a lot of time to get to the point where I could speak kind words to myself. The car wreck was unintentional, but it still inflicted so much damage and radical change in my life and in the lives of those around me. I was unknowingly suffering from post-traumatic stress disorder. I was argumentative and reactive, then I was indifferent and distance. I was not aware how my emotional instability was affecting those I was in a relationship with—family, friends, and especially my husband. One of the most painful emotions that I dealt with was shame. I experienced what is called survivor's guilt, which is the belief that the survivor could (and should) have changed the situation and prevented the outcome of the traumatic incident.

In Judith Herman's book *Trauma and Recovery: The Aftermath of Violence--from Domestic Abuse to Political Terror*, she discusses the concept of guilt for the survivors of trauma in the following sentences:

> In the aftermath of traumatic events, as survivors review and judge their own conduct, feelings of guilt and inferiority are practically universal... Guilt may be understood as an attempt to draw some useful lesson from disaster and to regain some sense of power and control. To imagine that one could have done better may be more tolerable than to face the reality of utter helplessness.[6]

The guilt I experienced was my attempt to regain some control—to make some sense of an event that caused so much pain. Many traumatized individuals believe on some level that they allowed, if not even encouraged, the traumatic event to occur. I felt this. The alienating effect of shame interfered with intimacy in many areas of my life: spiritually with God, sexually and emotionally with my spouse, and relationally with family and friends.

I needed the assistance of others to move out of this emotional place. Even though I felt I didn't deserve their support, I needed it. Finally, I allowed them into my dark prison of emotions and accepted their understanding. And this led me to gradually accept myself. I had to let others in and to acknowledge that I too had been injured notably from the psychological trauma from the accident. I learned to forgive myself for the hurt that occurred to people for whom I cared deeply. Learning to love and forgive ourselves is essential to be able to love others fully. Forgiving ourself produces value, worth and a person who is able to give and receive love.

RECONCILIATION

Forgiveness does not also always go hand in hand with reconciliation—for many reasons. A primary reason is if the offender continues to be damaging and abusive in our present day life. The harmful behavior needs to completely before any possibility of reconciliation can occur. Also, reconciliation does not necessarily mean we enter back into the same kind of relationship we had before. We may decide to have a more distant type of relationship.

When two people choose to reconcile, they often have to determine what it will look like and how close they will be during the process. Reconciliation does not mean everything returns to how it was before the damaging incident occurred. In fact, it rarely does. But often the people involved can find a different plane of relationship where they don't harbor hurts and find new ways of relating.

I am reminded of so many stories where instead of going through the process of reconciliation, people choose to either stay stuck in resentment or pretend the hurtful incident never happened. For real forgiveness to take place, it is imperative to identify and take ownership for how each individual has contributed to the problem, argument, or hurtful incident—excluding abuse—where the innocent, violated person has no fault.

It takes time and risk to find a new way of relating. I have heard people say when talking about someone they want out of their life, "Just ignore her, and she will go away." They simply want the problem gone without honoring the relationship and without the work of authentic forgiveness. This is in direct contrast to living the *aware life*. As author Paula Rinehart states, "We are not to let the relationship just fall by the way. How many cut-off family members and friends would be prevented if we were open and honest and tenacious about addressing problems between us?"[7]

Empathy for the one who hurt us does not justify the harmful action but, rather, gives us the ability to start seeing him or her through a different lens. Such empathy will help us move toward authentic forgiveness but is never meant to justify an offense. Empathy is a powerful tool to the one who has been offended. It releases the bitterness that binds us and sets us free to live and love fully. Even if people have been toxic in our life, we can forgive them and let them go from our life in the right way.

I recently attended a conference where Dr. Sue Johnson, the founder of Emotionally Focused Therapy, spoke. She said this about forgiveness. True and authentic forgiveness is when the one who is hurt speaks their pain without blame to the person who hurt them and then for the one who caused the hurt to respond in such a genuine and empathetic manner the hurt person can start to be comforted and heal. Then and only then can comfort and reconciliation begin.[8]

The element of time is also a significant contributor to forgiveness. This was the case with Beth. I was always hopeful that a friendship of some sort would be found after the years of healing passed. There had been limited communication between us since the car accident, and it always felt awkward. And her family held bitterness toward me, which made things even more strained. But Beth's recovery was remarkable. And despite some struggles with memory issues, she is still the same generous, loving person she always was.

A few years ago, I was visiting friends in Colorado. Beth was one I wanted to see. We prearranged a meeting at Starbucks to catch up and reminisce. I was anxious and excited to see old friends, especially Beth. I had hoped for the type of connection with her that could only come from authentic forgiveness in Beth's heart and self-forgiveness in mine. It had been ten years since the accident, and I had hoped for restored friendship in every one of those years. Would the connection we once shared be there, or would it need more time—more healing? And there she was, beautiful inside and out. Her eyes were bright and warm. Our conversation was easy and unremitting. The connection was being woven with each look and laugh we shared. And I realized my hope of restored friendship had come to pass. The wait had been well worth it.

ANOTHER SESSION WITH JOE

In conclusion of forgiveness, I want to go back to my client Joe, who began to struggle with homosexual feelings during his first marriage. "I thought this was going to go away," he said. His defensive walls isolated his perspective, and he was angry. I encouraged Joe to recognize the times when he made good choices when he did not respond in unhealthy ways to others or himself. I directed him to recount the times he made decisions that made him feel good about his journey and his progress. I wanted him to experience self-forgiveness and know grace instead of the shame and anger he had experienced during times of confusion about his sexuality.

Anger will only keep us stuck. I invited Joe to grieve, to process all his emotions, and to give himself grace. "Joe, can you take a deep breath, forgive yourself for the times you weren't honest, and allow the feeling of forgiveness to rush over you? Can you accept your limitations and see your value?" Then I concluded in some simple validating words what I truly meant: "Joe, you are a good man. Don't ever forget it." He looked at me, and he let the protective walls down enough to let the words spill into his heart. He sat there in silence, and the peace in the room was thick. Joe had started to understand himself and give himself the greatest gift, his own acceptance and forgiveness.

Later in our time together, Joe began to see his desire to be fully known had been deadened by his desire for a superficial acceptance. To be true to himself, he had to come to a place of peace. In the midst of his struggle, Joe started to accept himself—not because his battle went away but rather because it didn't. It's not always an easy road to navigate when values collide with desires, but he found that he was still freer and more fulfilled because he wasn't hiding anymore. Joe stated, "I'm okay with it [my sexuality] never being settled as long as I have peace." Joe continued, "I have come to see when I ask God, 'Why do I have this struggle?' I don't hear anything, but I am not turned off by God. And I know God isn't turned off by me, and somehow in that place I have peace. I have seen what lying and denying my sexual battle has done to me [severe depression and suicide], and I know that isn't God, and that isn't love."

DISCOVERY QUESTIONS: FORGIVENESS

Recommendation: Do Exercise VII - PRACTICE FORGIVENESS in Self-Awareness Exercises.

1. What is forgiveness to you?

2. Is forgiveness a choice? Why is choosing to forgive important as you intentionally pursue living the *aware life?*

3. Define each of the following options one can make regarding forgiveness:

    i. Forgiveness Refusal

    ii. Cheap Forgiveness

    iii. Authentic Forgiveness

4. Which one of these forgiveness styles do you prefer? Or do you experience all of them at different times?

5. Forgiveness is a process - so is reconciliation. Are there relationships in your life that need forgiveness? How about reconciliation?

6. How can self-forgiveness allow you to live the *aware life?*?

CHAPTER 8

GRATITUDE

As I have matured, I have come to see how important gratitude is to live a full and truly enlarged life. Seeing life through the perspective of thankfulness is not a delusional fantasy of instant happiness. It could mean we're enjoying the blessings we are receiving or that we are enduring hardships and struggles. In either situation, being thankful breeds contentment and calms the worries of our soul. I find those who have a rich foundation in being a generally grateful person are very attractive. Others flock to them, as they naturally exude peace and confidence. They usually have a good sense of humor as well and are able to laugh at themselves and make the most of difficult situations. Gratitude spills outward, and others are caught in its genuine, positive influence.

> *Reflect on your present blessings*
> *Of which every man has many -*
> *Not on your past misfortunes,*
> *Of which all men have some.*
> ~ *Charles Dickens* ~

Gratitude is the fourth and final key in journeying toward an intentional *aware life*. When we live in congruence to each of these pillars of optimism, humility, and forgiveness, we cultivate a life of gratitude. I am talking about the deep and spiritual thankfulness for every breath we take, every person we meet, every life season we live—the good, bad, and ugly. Gratitude is easy to express when something good happens and when we get what we want. But intentional gratitude is not based on the condition of our external world. It's in who we are—what we think and express. It's an intentional decision to see life through the lens of thankfulness. It is not focused on self but others. Author Deborah Norville in her book *Thank You Power: Making the Science of Gratitude Work for You* states, "Real gratitude is an others-focused emotion in which the emphasis is on the giver, not one's own betterment or psychic improvement. A what's-in-it-for-me attitude will probably leave you disappointed."[1]

> *It's an intentional decision to see life through the lens of thankfulness.*

"TWO-BY-TWO"

When I first moved into a smaller, charming house after my divorce, the yard was a mess. The weeds suffocated any grass that was trying to survive. Loving to work outside, I decided to start on the project of seeding my yard. So I went to Lowe's and bought the necessary ingredients: topsoil, grass seed, and peat moss. I then planted a section of the yard with the seed, watered it, and waited. Finally, the new, thin seedling began to appear, and I felt excited that in the midst of my weeds I was growing some grass. Real grass. It was green and lush. I loved to stand on it and feel the pride of bringing something new, something good, to my barren backyard. The only problem with this section of my soft, lush, green grass was that it only spread two feet by two feet. The rest of the yard hadn't taken the grass seed and remained dry, weedy, and barren. It wasn't much, but it was right outside my back door. When life got hard, I would go stand on my two-by-two yard and find comfort. I would look at the rest of the grass struggling to overcome the weeds and smile. I had a piece of goodness. I had a place for hope. In spite of everything else, I was grateful.

How can we find our two feet by two feet piece of grass? In life and in relationships, we have to look for the good, be thankful, and choose to love well, even if the goodness seems small compared to the weeds. Making the choice to be thankful gives us the energy and power to keep going and keep loving. Dreamer writes, "Finding courage to take another breath and not close my heart to myself or the world where there is pain is what I seek to learn—how to love well."[2] The key to choosing to love well and keeping our heart open is found in the attitude of gratefulness.

LIVE LIFE LOOSELY

To live in a manner that allows freedom of choice and avoids controlling behavior is *living life loosely*. It is a practice of living life with open hands—not grasping on to anything or anyone too strongly. The blessing we have today may not be here tomorrow. Living life loosely is a concept that fosters residing in the present. It encourages the attitude of being thankful for the present moment rather than dwelling on the past or worrying about the "what ifs" of the future.

Part of living life loosely goes back to the idea of healthy good-byes, as discussed earlier. When relationships come to an impasse, they often end badly. It is easier to leave with the power of anger than to bow out with integrity when a relationship, a job, or a situation just isn't working. But in the midst of anger and disappointment, we can act out in ways that are neither healthy nor caring.

It is a practice of living life with open hands—not grasping on to anything or anyone too strongly.

Holding on to a relationship for too long or giving up on a relationship too quickly can produce much hurt and resentment. Many times if a relationship ends badly—there are questions one may ask in an effort to make sense of what caused the demise of the relationship. In attempting to answer these issues, often people will jump to assumptions. These assumptions may include the belief that somehow, someway, we know more about the girlfriend or boyfriends' motive than the person ending the relationship does. We often assume the worst and believe we can read the other persons' mind. This allows us to stay in control, never fully grappling with the loss of the relationship.

A healthy ending to a relationship is one in which we wish the other well. Hurt can be expressed from both sides, but so can gratitude. Sometimes we have to let go of one part of our life order for the rest of it to show up. Trusting the process toward the *aware life* allows us to say good-bye to the ones who need to leave our life and to say hello to the people who need to come in.

IS ENOUGH…ENOUGH?

Wouldn't it be great to feel like we were not in need of anything? Like everything we had was enough? And, we were enough? Gratitude breeds these positive feelings. It is actually ingratitude that leaves us in a state of lacking. Ungratefulness is a catalyst to look for something else, something more—never being fulfilled with what we have, our relationships, possessions, finances, friends, or career. Cultivating the gratitude attitude is so imperative to overcoming addictions that it is a major theme in most twelve-step programs. All addictive behaviors come from a sense of deprivation, a feeling of lacking that a person believes can be filled with a substance, whether it's alcohol, drugs, shopping, sex, food, or relationships. The desire for more and more is insatiable, and enough is never enough.

Intentional gratitude fosters a true appreciation for what we do have. Ultimately, as we appreciate what we do have, we realize that our sense of lacking is, for the most part, an illusion. The richness of our soul is ultimately what brings us happiness. The Chinese Taoist philosopher Lao Tzu (sixth century B.C.) correctly proclaimed, "He who knows enough is enough and will always have enough."[3]

INTENTIONAL GRATITUDE

Intentional gratitude is a choice to be fully responsible for our life. It is choosing not to be dependent on others for our worth and happiness. The major downfall of interacting with others in a dependent manner is that dependency gives the other person an enormous amount of power. Those who live a reactionary lifestyle find that they are pulled more vigorously by life's ups and downs, depending on what others are doing around them. But those who live intentionally with purpose still may experience the ups and downs, but they also experience more stability. Their life's satisfaction is not based on what others are doing or not doing. Living in a grateful manner focuses us on the present and brings more consistent joy and satisfaction. When we cultivate gratitude, we facilitate a stable and positive frame of mind.

We typically want to see life as hills and valleys. Life is going well, so we are on a hill full of happiness, on top of the world. But when something hurtful or disappointing happens, that mountain experience soon becomes a dry valley. Feelings come and go like waves in the ocean. Author M.J. Ryan in her book *Attitude of Gratitude: How to Give and Receive Joy Every Day of your Life,* states,

> Happiness, anger, fear, love, thankfulness—they arise in response to some external or internal trigger and then subside. We feel angry, and then we don't. We are 'in love' and then we aren't. We feel thankful, and then it's over.[4]

We live on the mountain, fearful of the next valley, or we dwell in the valley, always prepared for the worst. Feelings toss us back and forth as tides in an ocean. So how do we avoid being a rag doll, tossed here and there by every emotion we encounter?

In an interview with Larry King, author Rick Warren used an analogy that resonated with me. Instead of seeing life in terms of hills and valleys, try to view life's journey as a set of railroad tracks.[5] Both tracks are going to the same place; one track represents the good things that happen in our life, and the other track represents the bad. Both the positive and negative events often occur simultaneously. One area of our life may be going really well, like our job or marriage or health. But at the very same time in another area, we are encountering trouble. On which portion do we want to dwell? Is it one or the other? We may prefer to see things in either-or categories or good and bad, never seeing the gray. Seeing life is lived more in the gray tones than black and white allows us to accept the imperfection of life. It has both good and bad occurrences, often at the very same time. When we start to accept the reality that most of life is lived in the gray, then life's disappointments don't produce such a sting. Relinquishing control comes from realizing life will always have both good and bad, and yet still we will be okay no matter the circumstance. This is the foundation of peace. Learning to acknowledge this truth is a powerful tool against anxiety and disappointment, the two biggest emotional rivals of thankfulness.

Gratitude develops with maturity. Seeing life as two railroad tracks running to the same destination helps stabilize our world and keep us in balance. Is the world a happy place or a place of pain and hurt? We know the answer to that question depends on our outlook on any given day. When we consciously cultivate a positive mindset, the outcome is joy and happiness.

RESPOND OR REACT?

Every situation allows us the opportunity to choose the manner in which we will answer. In a disturbing event, we have the choice to *respond or react*. Thinking about this choice, I am reminded of the quote attributed to Plato. "Be kind, for everyone you meet is fighting a hard battle."[6] It's true that everyone is, has, or will again be battling something in his or her life. Our boundaries and our attitude will determine our response to every situation. *Reacting* to an adverse circumstance usually doesn't end well. Reactions involve angry outbursts, sarcastic remarks, mean attacks, or more manipulative and passive expression of anger such as the silent treatment and guilt trips. Reactions may have different faces, but one thing they have in common is the damage they do to relationships and intimacy.

Responses, on the other hand, are genuine in not ignoring the situation but also in not attacking. Responding is stating how the actions or words of another have affected us. We can take care of ourself by giving responses which are direct and honest, but don't damage the relationship. And we get to walk away from the confrontation, feeling good about ourself. One of our spiritual tasks is to move beyond our purely emotional reactionary way of life and begin to cultivate healthy responses as *habits of the heart*, meaning we learn to love even when we don't "feel" loving, to be kind when we'd rather be surly, and feel grateful when we don't particularly feel like being thankful. In this way we turn feelings, which come and go, into conscious attitudes that we enact even if we don't "feel" like it.[7] Responses allow us to make decisions about how we want to handle an offense in a much more calculated and helpful manner. The decision of how we will act when something or someone disappoints us is a daily one. Will we choose to cultivate a positive attitude and gratefulness? Will we have the ability to respond versus react? What gets in the way of our responding more often? Is it a sense of entitlement, an angry heart, or a familiar pattern? I have found it is tough to have destructive reactions when we are nurturing a genuine attitude of gratitude in our life. In a nutshell, *reacting* destroys. *Responding* builds intimacy and self-efficacy.

A couple in their sixties came to my office for marriage counseling. They had been married for over forty years, and a pattern of reacting was embedded in the way they communicated. Dennis would do or say something that would irritate Ellen so she would explode into a rampage of abusive name calling and threats. It became too much for Dennis when she threatened to kill herself in one of her manipulative rages, so he called me. After getting Ellen on medication to regulate her moods, I began the work of teaching her new skills of responding, not reacting.

One visualization that helped Ellen when she started to feel anger was to see a bomb with a long wick. The longer the wick, the more time before the bomb exploded. As she visualized the wick being long, she was less impulsive and was able to express her frustrations in a healthier way. She was able to be more objective and remember the good things Dennis was doing which fostered a sense of gratitude. And this gratitude allowed the wick to get even longer. The ability to respond and not react was powerful in the way Ellen and Dennis related, so they both felt a greater satisfaction in their marriage.

BENEFITS OF INTENTIONAL GRATITUDE

When we choose to be grateful (rather than bitter) in response to a hurtful experience, we instantly feel the difference in our body and mind. We feel lighter, happier, and have more energy. Focusing on the positives brings incredible benefits. Being self-aware in who we are fosters the ability to be grateful for all that life has brought us, even when it comes in the form of loss and struggle. The emerging field of positive psychology focuses on the benefits of being grateful for what we have rather than concentrating on what we don't. For years science has looked at what happens to human beings when something goes wrong. We have heard of the negative effects of stress and anger on the cardiovascular system and immune system. But now research is identifying the benefits of possessing a *positive* outlook. Experiencing positive situations and recognizing them as such can result in a mass of hopeful outcomes ranging from fewer illnesses and higher immune responses to less conflict in relationships and more positive and creative thinking.

Being intentionally grateful allows us to:

- bounce back from adversity faster,
- be more joyful,
- have fewer illnesses and possibly live longer,
- be more optimistic,
- be more likely to help others,
- get more sleep and more exercise,
- be more organized and have less clutter, and
- even be more likeable.[8]

So are we ready to jump on the grateful bandwagon? We all should be. But it's one thing to want it, and it's another thing to do it… to take a complete look at ourself and then choose to cultivate gratitude. Seeing life as fluid can help we move out of negativity. What I mean by this is being able to see life as flowing, smooth, and graceful—free from obstructions. It's like the sensation of feeling water flow over our body. It's refreshing, always changing. When life isn't fluid, it's stagnant—like a murky pond in which we typically find ourself stuck. The key to seeing life as fluid is the ability to move from one compartment of our life to another without becoming fixated. We see life as a whole. We see all of it, not just the one area or areas of struggle. Intentional gratitude produces growth. There are new situations, new beginnings every day. Bad days and bad things occur, but life will bring something new. Gratitude is the bridge that allows us to focus and refocus on the positive.

We can gather the benefits of choosing a fluid, grateful life, starting right now. We have within us the tools to live the life of satisfaction, security, and optimism for which we long. Begin with two words: *thank you*. Norville explains;

> People in the worst imaginable situations seemed relentlessly optimistic. They looked for the better day to come and expected it with certainty. How was this possible? In each instance, it ultimately came down to the same answer: they were grateful. In each of their heartbreaking situations, they had found something for which they could be thankful, because being thankful was a long-held habit.[9]

Practicing gratitude, acknowledging the blessings in our life, and making it a point to recognize the good will positively change our life. We will be happier, healthier, and better able to handle the stresses of daily life simply by cultivating true and real gratitude.

GRATITUDE MEDITATIONS

Meditation is often used to decrease stress. This simple act will make us more alive, less frustrated and more aware of our thankfulness for the things and people in our life. Below is an example of meditation I often use with my clients. Incorporating meditations like this one into our everyday life and see how gratitude increases as stress decrease.

Try this meditation exercise to increase gratitude and decrease daily stress.

1. One, two or four times every day, slow down and bring your attention to your breathing.

2. Notice that your breath flows in and out without your having to do anything. Focus on your stomach, and as you inhale, allow the air to gently push your stomach out. As you exhale, consciously relax your stomach so that it feels soft.

3. Continue breathing this way for five slow, deep breaths.

4. Then for each of the next five inhalations, say the words thank you silently for reminding yourself of the gift of your breath and how blessed you are to be alive. Often people have a stronger response when they imagine their experience of gratitude centered in their hearts.

5. After the five breaths of thanks, return to the soft stomach breathing for another two breaths.

6. Then gently resume your regular activity.

DISCOVERY QUESTIONS: GRATITUDE

Do Exercise VIII - SELF-AWARENESS in Self-Awareness Exercises.

1. How can intentionality help you have a more grateful attitude?

2. What is the concept of "living life loosely?" Are there any areas in your life you think would help you if you applied this concept?

3. Have you felt like a rag doll tossed here and there by every emotion you encounter? How can gratitude be a grounding force to help stabilize your emotions?

4. Describe *Respond vs. React.*

a. Which behavior do you do more often-*Respond* or *React?*

b. In what situations are you more tempted to *React* instead of *Respond?*

5. How can you form the habit of gratitude in your everyday life?

PART 3

THE *AWARE* LIFE

CHAPTER 9
INTENTIONALITY

L iving the intentional *aware life* is a lifestyle. It's a decision we make over and over again. Dr. Brené Brown, a research professor, introduced this concept of the process in her insightful book *The Gifts of Imperfection*, where she writes, "Wholehearted living is not a one-time choice. It is a process. In fact, I believe it's the journey of a lifetime".[1]

The *aware life* has many facets, yet the one consistent factor in this journey is intentionality. To tap into the *aware life*, we must make the risk to be present, pay attention, and always, always, move forward.

> *To tap into the aware life, we must make the risk to be present, pay attention, and always, always, move forward.*

One of my favorite words is **resolve**, meaning "determination: a firmness of purpose."[2] Fulfillment requires resolve. It demands we make a choice, take action, and stay the course. I believe many people lack fulfillment in their lives because they do not choose to pay attention to how they live their life on a daily basis.

I don't think change magically happens. It takes awareness, determination, and conscious choice. Intentionality is connecting with our soul, then creating the life we are intended to live.

Having more fulfillment, joy, and purpose in our life begins with taking the time out of our busy schedule to be still and listen to our inner voice. Where does our mind go when we silence it from everyday tasks and our to-do list?

It is this silence followed by a determination that alters our journey. It's up to us; live a messy life asleep—unaware of our heart's desire, or live a messy life fully awake—aware of all that life has to give us. And the journey can be messy whether we choose to go through life asleep or if we elect to go through it awake and aware Intentionality makes the difference in the joy and fulfillment we can experience.

At fifty years of age, David realized his life was dull and his relationships unrewarding. I started coaching David on his life purpose and how he wanted to design his life. His job paid well, but he found it unsatisfying. His marriage was boring, and the temptation for a greener pasture was great—though he hadn't acted on it. And his spiritual journey and self-care had become parched and routine.

I gave David the homework of evaluating his current life with the life he wanted. We started with value clarification, life area fulfillment scale, and concluded with fulfillment work. Anyone can fill out a questionnaire or write out a goal, it takes intentionality to walk the path that brings about change.

David was one of the few who was determined to change his life for the better. He became intentional in his plan to change. And he was successful. After going through the self-awareness work, David realized his job did not utilize his natural ability to teach and help others. He took another job that gave him more satisfaction in what he valued. He also encouraged his wife to go through the same discovery process, and she eagerly agreed. Together they were able to recover a passionate and vibrant relationship.

The last part of David's journey to fulfillment was integrating a healthy amount of self-care into his life. He took a few fishing trips with friends and started to work out regularly. At the end of his process, he truly had the fulfilling life he wanted. David took the time to evaluate and purposefully live out his desire to change his life, his decision to do so brought long-lasting fulfillment and joy.

INTENTIONALITY IS NOT A TO-DO LIST

In her book, *Living with Intent*, Mallika Chopra states, "Intents aren't merely goals. They come from the soul, from somewhere deep inside us where we get clarity on our heartfelt desires for happiness, acceptance, health, and love."[3] They are inspirations that flow with energy from our soul. They are not a list of goals. They are you—the creative, on-purpose you.

Daily soul petitioning is required to bring meaning to each day. Through the process of pausing and reflecting, we set an intention, a purpose for the day, whether that is our health, relationship growth, or spiritual connection. All intentions mandate us to pause and listen to our heart. When we listen to our true calling for fulfillment, connection, and purpose, we can't but help to live with intentionality. Or we risk our soul sleeping away its purpose.

> *Intentionality is about learning how to identify who we truly are and to live out of that truth.*

Dr. Wayne W. Dyer, counselor and self-help author, states in his book, *The Power of Intention: Learning how to Co-Create Your World Your Way*,

Intentionality takes discipline, but it's not a to-do list. It's a choice to stop and pay attention to what is already there waiting for us. It's beckoning us to become aware. It's there always—waiting, calling, urging us to pause long enough to find our truth and embrace our passion.[4]

Intentionality is about learning how to identify who we truly are and to live out of that truth. It requires the ability to balance our life and know our self. One of the first truths we must embrace is that our ego is not us. When the ego is our focus, we do not see our true-self. We see an illusion of who we are—a manifestation of our need for self-importance and others' conditioning of our life. "Our ego is simply an idea of who we are that we carry around with us."[5]

Dr. Dyer gives seven steps for overcoming our ego:

1. Stop being offended. The behavior of others isn't a reason to be immobilized.

2. Let go of our need to win. Ego loves to divide us up into winners and losers.

3. Let go of our need to be right. Ego is the source of a lot of conflict and dissension because it pushes us in the direction of making other people wrong so we can be right.

4. Let go of our need to be superior. True nobility isn't about being better than someone else.

5. Let go of our need to have more. The mantra of the ego is more. It's never satisfied.

6. Let go of identifying ourself by our achievements.

7. Let go of our reputation. Our reputation is not located in us. It resides in the minds of others.[6]

    Dr. Brené Brown in her book, *The Gifts of Imperfection*, gives the reader a "let go" list. It's a list of ten guideposts for wholehearted living. Included in the list are "cultivating authenticity: letting go of what people think," and "cultivating creativity: letting go of comparison."[7] Concluding from Dr. Dyers and Dr. Brown's lists—there will be a lot of letting go, going on, to permit wholehearted intentional living. And I believe when wholehearted intentional living occurs, the *aware life* is evident.

INTENTIONALITY AND AUTHENTICITY

Authenticity! Now that's a word commonly being thrown about in our culture. It's a concept that demands we should know what it fully means and should know how to live it out. But I find it much more elusive than what most people think. Take Kim, for example. She continually finds herself in unfulfilling relationships with emotionally unavailable men. Why the pattern? Why doesn't she choose to find another type of man—an emotionally available one?

    When we are making choices from a subconscious pattern of thinking, it is nearly impossible to change behaviors. For change to occur, there must be two elements: **First**, there has to be the desire to do something different—to move away from the familiar. Though the familiar isn't always fulfilling, it's what is known—and the KNOWN is incredibly powerful. **Second**, do the work to become self-aware—through self-exploration, being present, and mindfulness.

    The journey toward self-knowledge is sacred. It's a journey where we ask ourselves the big questions.

- Who am I?
- What is my purpose?
- What is fulfillment to me?

Recognizing the life script we are living that no longer serves us, and choosing to change is bravery at its finest. On this journey, we also learn that although our life-view is entirely our own, our behaviors affects others. The intentional lifestyle requires self-awareness and authenticity, which ultimately demands self-responsibility.

For Kim, it was the realization that she was living out the wounds of her emotionally neglectful and abusive father, by choosing emotionally detached and verbally abusive partners. This realization was the beginning of her journey toward health and healing. Kim was now aware of her wounds and how they manifested in her relationships. The change in her life then became her self-responsibility.

RUN OUR RACE

The act of honoring our soul is part of the individuation process. It's a conscious spiritual enlargement of who we are, separate from others. The concept of individuation comes from psychologist Carl Jung. His idea of individuation summarized the lifelong project of becoming more and more the person we were meant to be. Not the person our parents, or our friends, or our community wants us to be. Or the person our frightened ego says we must be. It means just being the person we were intended to be—the original intent of self.

The original intent facilitates the creation of what we were intended to bring into this world. The essence of our intentional life is found in the process of individuation.

The thing that often causes unhappiness is an unhealthy attachment to a person or a thing. It's the clinging to the person or the object that causes the pain. Clinging is the outcome of the belief we will not be happy unless we have a particular person or object. Thus, we hang on with all our might. The fear of being without the person or object keeps us trapped.

It is often fear that prevents people from individuating from significant people in their life. They are terrified to lose their relationship or the approval they seek. Fear is the greatest reason to choose to go back to the familiar and stay numb—to slumber in history's unmade bed. To awaken to life and love is to see ourselves as complete and not needing others to fulfill us. We must chop off the part of our psychological self that has an unhealthy attachment.

In his book, *The Way to Love*, Jesuit priest and psychotherapist Anthony de Mello explains an unhealthy attachment,

> And what is an attachment? A need, a clinging that blunts your sensitivity, a drug that clouds your perception. That is why as long as you have the slightest attachment for anything or any person, love cannot be born.[8]

Individuation diminishes the power of what others want us to be—in personality, career, marriage, children, and beliefs. This process does not cut a person off from society. Rather, it cuts a person off from the superficial crowd, as it deepens genuine connection and authentic relationships.

Individuation demands we ask different questions. Instead of asking, "What do my parents, spouse, partner, friend, church, or community demand of me? What will please them?" We ask, "What is my life's intention? What will fulfill my creativity, my purpose, my passion and uphold my values?" The false gods of our culture, such as power, materialism, and self-centeredness, always diminish the original intent. Asking the harder questions we encounter in this book will stir up thoughts that will help us live more aligned with the original intent for our life.

In fact, if we don't have moments of confusion, doubt, or feeling "lost"—we are asleep or in the familiarity of autopilot. These uncomfortable feelings mean the subconscious is making

> *Journeyers realize their old ways aren't working anymore. They realize the bumps in the road reveal an unhealthy pattern and they take notice.*

its ways to the conscious. This recognition of emotional discomfort takes time; that's why most people start this journey of self-awareness after they have lived a few years and experienced a few bumps in the road of life.

Journeyers realize their old ways aren't working anymore. They realize the bumps in the road reveal an unhealthy pattern, and they take notice. The pattern might be in our relationships, work choices, or self-care. No matter which area of your life you see these self-defeating patterns—it is time to burst out and live your intentional life.

WANTS AND NEEDS—WHICH IS WHICH?

The confusion between wants and needs often causes havoc in people's lives. Tiffany came to my office with symptoms of chronic depression with frequent panic attacks. These attacks were often disabling. She would retreat to her bed for days following each of these panic attacks—feeling safety only in the comfort of her home and bed. Her depression would increase following these anxiety attacks and the consequential isolation.

The depression stemmed directly from the times of isolation where she would obsess about her feelings of loneliness. When she ventured out of her house, she would often find comfort in buying various inexpensive items at the Dollar Store, Walmart, and every garage sale she could find. The browsing and buying of dollar items collected in a jam-packed car and her home became full of boxes and unneeded items that stacked in every corner. Her hoarding problem grew with every day she continued this pattern. Tiffany was always one who had too much clutter, but her recent behavior of dulling her hurt through collecting and hoarding had a much more severe and damaging result.

The buying began innocently, she would tell herself she could use the items she was buying at her job as a school teacher. Later, her collecting became invasive and overtook every room in her home with a 5-foot pile of "stuff"—leaving only a narrow pathway to get from one room to another. One day in session, she asked if we could work on how she could fill this "need" to browse in healthier manners. She began to explore the difference between needs and wants. And browsing and buying dollar-store items did not fall into the "need" category.

In psychologist Abraham Maslow's hierarchy of needs, he postulated that each level of need had to be achieved before we can progress upward to a more evolved need.

- The first level of need is **physiological** (breathing, water, food, and sleep).

- The second level is **safety** (security of body, family health, and property).

- The third level includes **love/belonging** (friendship, family, and sexual intimacy).

- The fourth level is **self-esteem** (confidence, respect of others, and respect for others).

- The top level is **self-actualization** (creativity, lack of judgment of others, morality, and acceptance of facts).[9]

The three highest need levels are condensed efficiently into two categories:

- **Connection**—a healthy bond among family members, friends, partners, or a group that shares a mutual interest that facilitates peace, fulfillment, and joy in life.

- **Purpose**—the goal or intent of part or the whole of life.

Tiffany later came to recognize that her so-called "need" to browse and buy was a way to numb and medicate her true feelings. I asked her, "How does browsing help you get your true needs for purpose and connection?"

And a light bulb went off, as she recognized browsing was a "want" and not a "need." It was a temporary solution to a lifelong desire. The browsing and buying of small insignificant items ceased her loneliness and anxiety for the moment, but loneliness would return minutes or hours later with a fury.

Tiffany's hoarding behavior correlated directly to her anxious feelings. It took four months to de-clutter her home, and she had to daily, intentionally, choose to not bring more things into her home.

In counseling, she signed a contract with me that she would not go to a dollar store or a garage sale. The agreement helped her have accountability as she changed the way she thought and was intentional to live differently. Focusing on her actual needs empowered Tiffany to address the need for connection and purpose instead of burying them under a 5-foot pile of dollar store items.

THE BRAIN

What's great about change is that our brain adapts and makes new neural pathways as we repeat the same healthier behavior. In the outer layer of the brains, there are more than 100,000 miles of nerve fibers. This complete nervous system reaches to our skin. Millions of nerve endings of the skin sense tiny variations of light, sounds, vibrations, touch, smell, temperature, etc., and then transport this information to the brain.

The brain then processes this information in a millisecond and determines what to do next. The brain is the most responsive computer on Earth. The marvel of the brain is not just its capacity for holding knowledge, but how its sensitivity to stimuli teaches the body how to survive. Learning occurs when the body predicts something will happen based on memory in the nerve and, therefore, controls the outcome.

The irony of the brain is that the more we learn, the less we need the brain. The brain can be put into a sleep state—figuratively speaking. As soon as the brain can consciously and subconsciously predict what is going to occur, it doesn't have a need to learn more. The desire to grow, to learn, and to explore is a blessing. It's this continuous state of uneasiness that keeps the brain operating as it is meant to function.

It's this continuous state of uneasiness that keeps the brain operating as it is meant to function.

Often resolutions, such as losing weight, getting out of debt, or exercising more, fail when there is a similar pattern in how they come to their dismissal. When we start, we experience success, but when it gets harder and harder, we start to cheat or give ourselves permission to not follow the plan. Then within a few weeks after the cheating, we go back to our old ways entirely.

What happens is not our lack of resolve; rather it is an issue that arises from our faulty thinking. We believe if we succeed in losing weight, becoming debt free, or getting on a regular exercise program, our whole life will change for the better. When our life doesn't improve as quickly as we expected, we get disheartened and relapse to old habits.

To change behaviors for good, we have to do brain work. We have to actually "rewire" our brain. In the intriguing Charlie Rose YouTube *Brain Series*, scientists such as Antonio Damasio, Kerry Ressler and Joseph LeDoux discuss the use of magnetic resonance imaging (MRI) to identify thinking patterns that cause habitual behavior. These patterns are called neural pathways or neural memories.[10]

People will always default to their "known" or "familiar" behavior and thinking. Thus, trying to change our default *behavior* by going to our default *thinking* just strengthens the pathway. True change can only happen when we create new neural pathways from new ideas.

So let's be gentle with ourselves; we didn't get our go-to behavior overnight, and the change we want to make in our life will take time also. New neural pathways need to be strengthened with time and with practice. In essence, change requires new thinking.

So, here are a few tips to help start the journey toward an intentionally *aware life*:

1. Choose one area you would like to change.

2. Set specific goals—make them realistic.

3. Don't forget to give yourself a pat on the back and congratulate yourself for success with any and every milestone achieved.

4. Change your thinking about the behavior you want to change. Practice it in your mind, see yourself doing the behavior that is more efficient or looking the way you wish to look.

5. Don't get ahead of yourself: focus on today and stay present.

THE 80/20 RULE

A standard yet faulty approach to living with intentionality is "all or nothing" thinking. We start off with determination and zeal to change an aspect (or aspects) of our life, but 15, 30, 60 days later we are back to the way we were living before. It's the New Year's resolution syndrome all over again. We plan to lose weight, get a better job, declutter our house, start a fitness program, eat whole foods, have more fun, enhance our marriage, and so on and so on.

What accounts for the high rate of failure? Are people just lazy? Or do they really don't want to change?

I find it's neither. People tend to be lazy at times, but that's not the reason resolutions are unsuccessful. And, after twenty-plus years of being a therapist, I honestly can say people *do* want to change, but they just don't have the tools or the support to be successful.

The setting of resolutions and the consequential failure to keep them is a cultural phenomenon of these days. People desire to reinvent themselves but haven't considered if they are ready for the change. People set unrealistic goals about their resolutions, and then when the resolution becomes unattainable, not only does the resolution fail, but they feel like they failed. That damages their self-esteem.

When the results are not as evident or as easy as we had hoped for, it's easy to give up. That's why I live by and counsel others to live by the 80/20 rule. This rule requires us to live in an intentional manner toward a goal 80 percent of the time, while 20 percent of the time we give ourselves grace.

For example, we want to start eating healthier foods, cutting out the fast foods, and eating whole foods—fruits, veggies, etc. We are doing well until the day comes when we just don't have the time to make a healthy dinner, and we're starved. So, we drive through a fast food restaurant and order a hamburger and fries, allowing that meal to be in the 20 percent. This approach keeps us out of the "all or nothing" mentality that typically leads to failure.

We can also do this in other areas of our life—as long as we stay consistent with our goal and remain on the path of desired change. One more important aspect of change is belief—we must believe we will be able to change our attitude, behavior, or habit. Then we choose to act in the manner towards success, believing we will meet our goals. Finally, honor and congratulate yourself as you courageously create new pathways of living your fulfilled life. Don't demand perfection—give yourself lots of grace, but stay intentional.

DISCOVERY QUESTIONS: INTENTIONALITY

Recommendation: Do Exercise IX - YOUR *AWARE LIFE* DEFINED in Self-Awareness Exercises.

1. Intentionality is a lifestyle. It is not a to-do list or a goal. It comes from within and is the purposeful manner we choose to live our life. How can you create an intentional lifestyle in your life?

2. What does it mean to you to run your own race?

3. To cling to a person or an object for security is a certain sign of dependency. Do you struggle with needing someone or something too much to make you feel content?

4. Do you get confused at times and think something you need is just something you want or vice versa? What is an example of when you did this?

5. How would you use the 80/20 rule to help you succeed in reaching a goal you set? Pick an area you would like to be intentional to change.

CHAPTER 10
FULFILLMENT

WHAT IS FULFILLMENT?

We all probably have an idea of what goes into the *aware life*. Shelves of bookstores are dedicated to books and journals about the search for this concept. There are many modern definitions of purpose, meaning, and happiness—which are all elements of the *aware life*. But the definition that is most important is the one that resonates with you.

> *Fulfillment is saying yes to all that we are and then connecting with the ones who bring out our brilliance.*

Fulfillment is tied intimately to this concept of the *aware life*. Fulfillment is saying yes to all that we are and then connecting with the ones who bring out our brilliance, those few (and we only need a few) who say yes to our possibilities and talents.

Each and every person has his or her definition of fulfillment. I recently asked friends, family members, and clients their definitions. Here are some of the answers I received:

- Fulfillment… I think of the people in my life. First and foremost my kids and what I am able to do and have done for them and all that I get back from them. The same with my husband, my family, friends, and my clients. So, fulfillment to me is making a difference in someone's life and giving a part of myself. It means balance, peace, giving, accomplishment, joy, and to be loved. Sometimes I think being fulfilled is accepting where you have been and where you are now. And to continue to grow as a person and find the things that bring you joy. Being content, satisfied, and at peace with yourself is fulfillment.

- Fulfillment to me is the attainment of certain goals and needs. Whether attaining fulfillment comes consciously or unconsciously depends on the need or want. I'm fulfilled of my need for love through the relationships I have with my parents, siblings, and loved ones.

- Fulfillment to me is realizing my devotion to the One who created me. It's knowing why I get up every morning and my opportunity to have a positive impact no matter what job I am doing.

- Fulfillment means realizing your true purpose in life, being satisfied with it, and devoting every aspect of your being to achieving it.

- The word *fulfillment* to me is a feeling of arriving at a place that you always hoped you'd be—whether that be physically, emotionally, monetarily, spiritually or otherwise. I think when you are fulfilled, you come to a feeling of ease and a place of rest where you are able to breathe a little easier, things aren't as hard.

- Fulfillment: A glass completely full, but not spilling over. Busyness does not equal fulfillment; it is purpose actualized. Prior discernment of one's purpose is required before truly finding fulfillment.

Just as fulfillment is defined in so many unique ways, such is the same as the *aware life*. Though each answer varies, there are similar components. Each definition incorporates the ability to be intentional and authentic in relationships, work, and self-care. I would argue that while each person's definition of fulfillment may vary, the one essential component is knowing we are being genuine and true to who we are and "on task" being intentional in how we live. There is no way to feel fulfilled when living someone else's life.

LETTING GO

"I am so lonely," Jodi began. "I love the comforts of my life, but I feel they don't give me the joy I thought they would." This is how our first coaching session began. Jodi wanted the "*good life*" that included designer clothes, a more luxurious car, and, of course, a bigger house. She thought these things would fulfill her and make her happy, but they didn't. Jodi found the aching loneliness crept back in with a vengeance after each purchase. The initial high would quickly vanish, tempting her to buy again. With her growing despair, she was constantly on a pendulum between a life of depression and isolation and a life of quick-paced, impulsive adventure. She had not found a sense of contentment. She yearned for something more that would make her feel good—or at least not so sad. Jodi came to realize, as our coaching sessions progressed, that she was looking in the wrong place for fulfillment. She was looking outward—to things, to people, to anything that would make her feel like she had arrived and was finally alive, to things that would eventually and always disappoint. Her work was to move inward and discern who she was—to find herself again—and find who she was created to be.

Jodi began the intentional journey of unmasking her life and seeing the whys behind her actions. She needed to identify the ways in which she had pursued an inauthentic form of expressing her longings. As I have mentioned before, many times the journey starts with experiencing pain. Knowing where to go requires understanding where we have been—and from what we are running. As we explored Jodi's pain around her parent's divorce, her absent father, broken dreams, and hurtful relationships, she ultimately found peace. She had to de-clutter her soul before she could find real purpose and connection in her life,

ENERGY DRAINERS

The most common obstacles to living a fulfilling life come from energy drainers—those mental vampires (like clutter) that suck the vitality out of our days. Energy drainers come in two different forms. One is *little annoyances.* These are the small things that we usually brush off and ignore, unaware that they drain our attention and energy. Some examples of these annoyances can be messy closets and work shelves, a crowded garage, an unfinished or forgotten project. Most of us tend to tolerate these things until they accumulate too much.
Then we get so frustrated with these little annoyances that we may start working on them. If not, with time, they may become more substantial.

At that point, they may have moved to the next, more damaging form of energy drainers. These are the significant or *chronic complaints* that cause suffering. They create tension and literally crowd our worlds. We are aware of how they diminish the quality of our lives, but we usually just accept them, mostly because we do not know what to do about them. Examples of this type of energy drainer are long work hours, health issues, and harmful relationships.

They drain time that could be used to connect with others, or even to take care of ourselves. It is when activities like exercise become a thing of the past, and we can't recall our last vacation. Chronic complaints could be the demands of work, church, volunteerism, even family. Maybe your son says, "You never come to my baseball games, Dad!" or your elderly mother needs more care than you have been able to give, or that pile of papers in your office just keeps growing.

When our life aligns with our values and free of energy drainers, we can experience fulfillment daily.

AUTHENTIC SPIRITUALITY

Closely joined with fulfillment is the resurgence of personal spirituality. The recovery of a mature spirituality is one of the most challenging tasks of our time not only because there are so many distractions but because we flee from being utterly responsible for our experience. The negative heritage of being inundated with what others want from us continues to be disempowering. We abandon the pursuit of unrelenting reflection on the life of the spirit and choose the familiar and known. We choose black and white thinking instead of compromise, creative solutions, and interpersonal insight; thus we limit ourselves. I would propose that the secret to authentic spirituality is to live a grateful and fully *aware life*, being spiritual in ways that don't commonly look very spiritual.

In his book *Blue like Jazz*, Donald Miller introduced the term Christian spirituality, a nonpolitical, mysterious system that can be experienced but not explained.[1] This concept of God resonates with many who align with Judeo-Christian beliefs but have struggled with religiosity. Sometimes finding a right term that fits us gives the freedom and definition to be who we are. To live an enlarged, spiritual, and fulfilled life we have to listen to the longings of our heart. And in the listening, the answer is found.

I would offer that just as our definitions of ourselves are too small and confining, so our definition of God is too small. To believe God is bigger, better, and more real than tradition is an exciting concept. As James Hollis proclaims in his book *Finding Meaning in the Second Half Of Life: How to Finally, Really Grow up*,

> Growing up spiritually means that we are asked to sort through the possibilities for ourselves, find what resonates for us, what is confirmed by our experience— not the consensus of others—and be willing to stand for what has proved true for us. For this reason, the twin tasks of finding personal authority and finding a mature spirituality are inextricably linked.[2]

DEEP CHANGE

Living from the deep place is not easy to maintain. Our world is full of distractions—television, e-mail, Facebook, cell phones, and even our job, family, marriage, and friendships—are all bidding for our time and attention. This multi-tasking fosters compartmentalization and inhibits depth and quality of life. Living from a deep place may require us to undergo deep change. As Robert E. Quinn, organizational behavior and human resource management expert and consultant writes:

Ultimately, deep change is a spiritual process. Loss of alignment occurs when, for whatever reason, we begin to pursue the wrong end. This process begins innocently enough. In pursuing some justifiable end, we make a trade-off of some kind. We know it is wrong, but we rationalize our choice. We use the end to justify the means. As time passes, something inside us starts to wither: We are forced to live at the cognitive level, the rational, goal-seeking level. We lose our vitality and begin to work from sheer discipline. Our energy is not naturally replenished, and we experience no joy in what we do. We are experiencing slow death . . . We must recognize the lies we have been telling ourselves. We must acknowledge our own weakness, greed, insensitivity and lack of vision and courage. If we do so, we begin to understand the clear need for a course correction, and we slowly begin to reinvent our self.[3]

THE *AWARE LIFE*

The *aware life* and with it personal fulfillment comes from living with intention. The *aware life,* even a messy one, brings more significance, fulfillment, and meaning to life. It is living openly, authentically, and purposefully to satisfy every facet of our life. The longing for an enlarged life – a life embracing more possibilities, growth, and freedom is many times the catalyst to choose this intentional journey toward the *aware life*.

I often see people live their life in the opposite direction of what works. They try to have more things or more money to do more of what they want so that they will be happier. But often it's the opposite that works. We must first be who we genuinely are. Then go from there to do what we need to do to have what we want. The journey begins, as I have stated earlier, with the choosing to be present and grow in self-awareness, understand why we do what we do, and lastly intentionally change behaviors and attitudes that don't align with who we truly are. Living with intention and purpose is not always as easy as it sounds, but it is surely worth it.

> *The longing for an enlarged life – is many times the catalyst to choose this intentional journey toward the aware life.*

THERE ARE SEVEN CHARACTERISTICS OF THE *AWARE LIFE.*

- Give Freely and Generously.

Give your time, your money, your attention. Give of yourself. You will never regret the time you did something for another human being.

- Self-Care.

Don't forget to take care of yourself, spend some time alone, get a massage, read a book, and go on a solo-trip. See what it's like to vacation alone. Rejuvenate your energy. Don't listen to the old tapes that say you are selfish – indulge yourself every once in a while and – enjoy!

- Be Intentional about your Daily Choices.

Every choice, small or large needs to be made with thought and mindfulness. How you spend your time and who you spend it with is vital to how much fulfillment you experience in your life. Choose wisely!

- Love Fully.

Don't be embarrassed to show that you love or appreciate those in your life. Love out loud and you will never regret the words you never said.

- Go on Adventures and Build Memories.

There is nothing more fulfilling than sharing experiences with someone you love. Adventures give life to the mundane, walking up all your senses. Go on an adventure, have some fun, and take a risk to explore life outside of your comfort zone.

- Be an Optimist!

Choose the glass half full point of view in life, and see how much more fulfilled you will be.

- Lastly, be Yourself - do your own thing – just do it with kindness!

DISCOVERY QUESTIONS: FULFILLMENT

Recommendation: Do Exercise X - ENERGY DRAINERS in Self-Awareness Exercises.

1. What is your definition of fulfillment?

2. What does *authentic spirituality* mean to you?

3. How does intentionality influence fulfillment?

4. Write what the seven characteristics of the *aware life* mean to you personally below:

    - Give Freely and Generously:

    - Self-Care:

- Be Intentional about your Daily Choices:

- Love Fully:

- Go on Adventures and Build Memories:

- Be an Optimist:

- Be Yourself:

5. As you review the seven characteristics of the *aware life* - which one(s) will be the most challenging to you?

CHAPTER 11
FINDING ME AGAIN

Often the whole concept of discovering our true authentic self is viewed as foreign. Or selfish. Yet this process is vital to the *aware life*. The *aware life* is a cornucopia of humility, intentionality, and awareness; demanding vulnerability and honesty to grow and allow others to know us fully. It is an intentional process—sometimes done on our own, sharing the journey with those closest to us as we progress, and other times helped along by a mentor, counselor, or coach. Either way, the course of awareness is fundamental to living the life we want to live.

People have a unique ability to compartmentalize their lives. It's a way to keep things moving smoothly and attend to one event, one item, at a time. Unfortunately, we don't realize there is only one actual compartment: our true-self. When we lose our passion and purpose to keep functioning, we become robots with to do lists.

The real ability to connect with another person in a sincere and intimate manner resides in loving and knowing ourself. Only then can we genuinely offer all we are to those in our life. It sounds paradoxical, but we cannot fully love someone until we have grown to care and love ourself. Deliberate care of our soul is honoring ourself, allowing us to honor others. Only through self awareness can this occur.

EMOTIONAL INTELLIGENCE

In Dr. Daniel Goleman's words, emotional intelligence is "the capacity for recognizing our own feelings and those of others, for motivating ourselves, for managing emotions well in ourselves and in our relationships."[1] Displaying the elements that are so important in emotional intelligence—such as emotional self-awareness, empathy, and influence—is necessary also to the *aware life*.

Goleman makes a profound illumination when he says that emotional intelligence is anchored in self-awareness. Those who communicate most effectively by honoring their needs and don't make others responsible for meeting them are typically the most successful individuals, personally and professionally. In his book *Emotional Intelligence,* Daniel Goleman reveals that 80 percent of success in the workplace is primarily based on emotional intelligence, versus 20 percent based on IQ or smarts.[2] I believe that the statistics can be broadened to personal/relationship success. So if emotional intelligence is a key indicator for success, then why aren't more people trying to learn how to do better? If we are not one of those few who have a natural, God-given personality that oozes of emotional intelligence, then what do we need to do to learn how to gain it?

Living the *aware life* happens when we intentionally decide to raise our self-awareness, increase our emotional intelligence, and choose to love. The following are tools to continue fostering

> *Living the aware life happens when we intentionally decide to raise our self-awareness, increase our emotional intelligence, and choose to love.*

self-awareness. They will help us know our inner voice; then courageously journey to our true-self.

START THE JOURNEY

I hope by the time you have read this far in my book you have started and are fully engaged in the journey of self-awareness. But if not, it's not too late to start this journey. Being aware of our emotions and their effects, learning how to manage them, and becoming flexible with new ideas are all a part of the awareness process. So is becoming aware of what our life is lacking. Through my personal self-awareness process, I realized my life lacked several things that were important to me. The chaos of life had limited my passions— I had sacrificed many things I truly enjoyed and loved all to make peace with the demands of my life. I found myself becoming tired, indifferent and lost.

My client Stephanie was experiencing a similar fatigue and hopelessness. As a dedicated mother, Stephanie had devoted her energy and talents for her children. But had she surrendered too much? Squelching her dream of becoming an artist due to the demands of being a mom of three was only part of the issue. She gladly gave to her children, but it was her husband with his subtle manipulation that made her feel she wasn't a good mother and all she did was never enough. She did not call me for an appointment because of chronic depression or anxiety, but because of the vast difference between the superficial life she was living and the genuine life for which she hoped.

As I coached Stephanie, she became aware of her true-self. She discovered a way to honor her love for her family with the respect for herself. We worked on setting boundaries with her manipulative husband and saying no to him and to the children without guilt. She found her values of integrity and honesty, to be lacking and set out to correct them. Stephanie's family had to adjust to her new passions and love of painting—and with time, they did. "I finally gave up all that I thought I was supposed to be and allowed myself to do what I wanted. And now I have energy for both my family and my art."

PURPOSE WORK

When I talk to clients about defining their life purpose, many times they confuse life purpose with vision and mission. So before we discuss purpose work, I'll explain the difference.

Life purpose is the personal objective we pursue throughout our lifetime; it is a particular way of being for which we are designed. A *mission* is the way or ways we choose to fulfill our purpose at a particular point in our lives. For example, an individual whose life purpose is to "respect and incite the utmost and best in herself and others" could fulfill this mission through many different kinds of work and actions over the course of her life. *Vision* refers to a particular, compelling image of the future that an individual holds. Life purpose is found when we identify what gives us joy, contentment, and energy.

Questions to ponder:

- When do you feel most energized?
- What do you want to have more of in your life?
- What do you want to have less of in your life?

This process of deciding what we want to keep in our life and what we want to relinquish awakens the brain to a new way of thinking. If the answers came quickly, our life purpose is so near to bursting out. If its more of a struggle to find our purpose—I suggest setting aside intentional time daily to ponder the above questions. Journaling can be so helpful as ideas come to you. Write them down and review them often. See if the answers resonate with you over time. Also, doing the self-awareness exercises in the back of the book will be very helpful to bring clarity to you and your life purpose. Our purpose is probably something we have had for a while even though it may seem fragmented and unclear now. That is why doing self-awareness work to identify the times in our life when we felt energized when we were living our life's purpose is vital.

When we lose track of ourselves and only live according to what we do instead of who we are, we are living "off purpose," and life feels less fulfilling. We may feel apathetic as if we are only surviving, lacking passion. These times of discouragement or lack of fulfillment come in common seasons of life such as:

- Experiencing midlife (feeling listless, fatigued, disenchanted)

- Encountering losses (such as friendships/relationships, deaths, job loss, or health issues)

- Undergoing significant life transitions (children leaving, retirement, divorce, relocating home and life)

- Feeling a grave discrepancy between current work/role and the profound desire for self-purpose.

- Feeling overwhelmed with life and asking, "Is this how I really want to live?"

JOURNALING

Journaling is the most common tool in a therapist's bag, primarily because it works. If we pick up a pen and piece of paper when something is bothering us, journaling will reveal our true thoughts and feelings. It forces our hand to tell the truth about our heart. I have seen clients gain incredible insights when they took the time to write about something that had hurt them in the past, something that was frustrating them in the present, or something they were fearful about in the future. Often clients don't want to try this exercise, but they see the significant benefits as soon as they do. In reality it can be about the best and least expensive therapy there is.

Journaling is not like any other kind of writing. It's not an essay or letter although it may be written in that form. It's not a scholarly paper in any manner. It's liberated in structure and thought. Grammar and other confinements are thrown out the window. We remove ourself from the box and give freedom to express and release our heart onto the paper. There is no audience and no intimidation. It's just you and a blank sheet of paper, awaiting your soul.

It helps to write out all that makes us anxious and the worst of all we think. It releases, for lack of a better fitting word, the *yucky* part of us, never to be seen by anyone else and never allowed to bring us embarrassment. Journaling can also give wings to the dreams we have tucked deep inside. It is safe, and it belongs only to us.

WELLNESS

Focusing on obtaining a better quality of life is a prime example of intentional self-aware living. Wellness is one vital key in living a full life. Often it just takes a small but sustainable change in lifestyle to make significant mental or health improvements. Choosing to make one simple change can promote a more energetic and joyful life. This change can alter our entire life—for the better. This is especially true in the concept of wellness. Charles B. Corbin of Arizona State University who gives this definition of wellness: "Wellness is a multidimensional state of being describing the existence of positive health in an individual as exemplified by quality of life and a sense of well-being."³ The primary top-

> *"Wellness is a multidimensional state of being describing the existence of positive health in an individual as exemplified by quality of life and a sense of well-being."*

level dimensions of wellness include mental, physical, spiritual, social and lifestyle. A healthy balance in these dimensions results in the overall feeling of a good quality of life.

WELLNESS DIMENSIONS

1. MENTAL WELLNESS

The mental aspect of wellness includes developing a healthy personal way of life, maintaining a learning capacity and establishing healthy positive thinking. To assess our mental wellness, we can simple count and compare the number of happy and satisfied days compared to sad, depressed or unsatisfied days.

2. PHYSICAL WELLNESS

Are we healthy, free of sickness, in good shape? How is your weight? Need to lose a few pounds? Or gain some? Physical wellness is an intentional approach to avoid disease and sickness. The benefits of physical wellness are health and energy. This preventative approach includes: eating whole foods, drinking plenty of water, exercising to promote strength and flexibility, and maintaining a healthy weight.

3. SPIRITUAL WELLNESS

Becoming aware of our spirituality can increase peace, awareness, connectedness, and purpose. The spiritual aspect of wellness includes knowing our life's purpose, and intentionally developing our talents and gifts in a positive way. Using our values and gifts is deeply fulfilling and spiritually satisfying.

4. SOCIAL WELLNESS

Relationships have a drastic effect on our wellness. How we get along with our partners, family, friends, and co-workers add to our quality of life or dramatically takes away our fulfillment. The quality of our relationships with friends, family, neighbors and coworkers can have a dramatic effect on our wellness. Choosing to foster relationships that are healthy and bring goodness to our life, while choosing to let others go is an ongoing process in maintaining social wellness. Social Wellness also begs each of us to evaluate our involvement in the community we live in, and the world we inhabit.

5. LIFESTYLE WELLNESS

The lifestyle element of wellness includes work, recreation, and the home environment. There's an old saying that goes; "If we love what we do, we'll never work a day in your life." Those who love what they do can tell we there's plenty of truth to the saying. As most of us will spend more than half our lives at work, what we do at work matters immensely to our wellness. A healthy balance of relaxation time, fun, and play intermixed with work and purpose is essential to feeling well. And finally, there's the home environment. Our home, the surrounding area we live in, is critical to bringing us peace and security. Our lifestyle of how we spend money and our time can add to or distract from our personal or family wellness.

Wellness is an intention. It doesn't just happen. It is the deliberate reaching and maintaining of a certain level of health and life satisfaction. Defined wholly by us and our desires. Everyone is different. When we live the *aware life,* we are intentionally "on purpose" for each dimension of wellness.

SHARING THE JOURNEY

Sharing something with another—a failure, struggle, loneliness, sadness, even a dream—can be a fearful experience. We desire to connect, but we are afraid we will be judged, ridiculed, abandoned, or dismissed. We long to see if the awareness we have uncovered in ourself will be affirmed and embraced by others. We desire to be loved and accepted when we share our discoveries. If our findings are met with disapproval and judgment, we will most likely feel hurt, but at this time we have the opportunity to give ourself the acceptance and empathy that no other can. Internationally-known life coach and author Patrick Williams states, "Self-empathy can be recovered when we begin to look at ourselves—especially at the child we once were with the loving eyes of an accepting adult."[4] As we journey, we'll find the patience we will need to give ourself grace. Some people may not want us to change. They are comfortable with who we are because they know what to expect. Friends, spouses, children, bosses, pastors, etc., want the familiar even though they have heard this growth can breed more intimacy and connection in relationships and a deeper more fulfilling life.

Finding genuine support is essential as you continue the journey of growth toward your true-self. It is important to seek out those people who choose to love and embrace all of you. You hopefully learned from many sources, including this book, you must honor your heart and your voice. No longer can you settle for less. The *aware life* comes down to this: Will you live with integrity toward your life and yourself?

WRAPPING IT UP

OPTIMISM

Optimism is not only the springboard to the *aware life*, but it is the constant that keeps fulfillment a tangible reality. With a positive outlook, we possess a belief in positive outcomes for our life and our circumstances. It believes in the future, believing in ourself, and—believing in grace and goodness.

HUMILITY

Humility comes out of the place of being honest with ourselves. To participate in healthy relationships, we have to embrace fully who we are, the good and the bad. No one is perfect, but there is strength and beauty in all of us. Courage is humbly facing our flaws. Humility breeds peace, healing, and intimate and deep connections—all necessary for fulfillment. It also forces us to drop our masks. There is freedom in accepting our weaknesses and coming to terms with who we are. It's hard to feel fulfilled otherwise. The *aware life* doesn't mean being perfect or having a perfect life. But it does mean we are fulfilled by the presence of humility and genuineness found by being self-aware.

FORGIVENESS

Through humility, we gain forgiveness. We cannot be peaceful when holding resentment towards others. Fulfillment and bitterness won't coexist. But when we forgive, when we can accept the truth of who we are and who others are—that is when we know and experience fully living with peace and purpose. Withholding forgiveness confines us to a small space of living. And it is not until we let go of the angry parts of our heart that we can grow and experience freedom ourselves… the freedom that we thought we were holding over someone or something else, the freedom that was—in reality—ours.

GRATITUDE

Gratitude alone can change our life. Life can be messy—really messy—but gratitude helps us accept it just as it is. Gratitude keeps things simple when our worries and uncertainties seem so big. As we search our life and become aware of what it has given us, life becomes fuller and richer. We are thankful for the good, acceptant of the bad, and in the end, we find the fulfillment for which we long.

AN INVITATION

In writing the final chapter of this book, I had a conversation with Beth - my friend who was in the car wreck with me. She had known me for many years. As we were visiting, she made the observation that I was "Nancy again." I was once again the person she had known before I lost myself in a pursuit of pleasing others some years prior. I had become a chameleon, seeking the approval of others—losing the freedom of being myself. I didn't realize it as it was happening, but looking back now... I see the slow fade. The move, the new job, the marriage, the attitude... I don't know if any of it was ever right because ultimately it made me lose myself. Still, would I take any of it back? Maybe some. But ultimately all that matters now is I realize who I am and the life I want to live. And Beth gave me the greatest gift by recognizing this in me as well.

The journey toward the *aware life* is rich in truth and grace. No matter where we have been, it is not too late to return to where we know we want to be. Yet, it's not something that just happens. We have to be intentional, resolved, purposeful. But there is no better journey to begin with than the journey to finding ourself.

I wish you, fellow journeyers, peace and patience as you begin—or as you continue this journey towards the *aware life*. I wish you truth as well—truth about who you are, what gives you joy, energy, and makes you feel centered and inspired. How you can best give of yourself to bring more love into your life and the lives of those your touch. I invite you to be the most intentional self-aware person *you* can be and add to life's beauty.

DISCOVERY QUESTIONS: FINDING ME AGAIN

Recommendation: Do Exercise XI -WELLNESS QUESTIONNAIRE in Self-Awareness Exercises.

1. "You cannot fully love someone until you have grown to care and love yourself. Intentional care of your soul is honoring yourself, as you honor others."

    a. Have you found this to be true?

    b. Have you had a relationship in which you were not genuine and acted like someone you weren't – knowingly or unknowingly? What was the outcome of that relationship?

2. Managing and being aware of your own feelings is the first step to what Daniel Goleman has coined Emotional Intelligence (EQ) *"the capacity for recognizing our own feelings and those of others, for motivating ourselves, for managing emotions well in ourselves and in our relationships."*

    a. Is *Emotional Intelligence* a strength for you or a growth area?

    b. How can learning to monitor your responses facilitate better relationships?

3. What do you want to have more of in your life?

4. What do you want to have less of in your life?

5. What does the *aware life* look like to you now? Is it different from what you thought before you read this book?

* Take Exercise XII - FULFILLMENT 30 POSTTEST in the Self-Awareness Exercises.

I hope you are excited to see how much your score has improved by doing the *aware life* work.

And lastly...congratulations for showing up, staying present, and intentionally choosing to be *aware!*

Nancy

DEAR READER

I encourage you to go through the Self-Awareness Exercises to gain more insight. Share these insights with your group, a wise friend, a mentor, or a professional counselor or coach to help you achieve and maintain the growth you desire.

ALL THE BEST!

NANCY

SELF-AWARENESS
EXERCISES

EXERCISE I: FULFILLMENT 30 PRETEST

Take this quiz to see how fulfilled your life is prior to doing the following exercise. You will get a chance to take it again after you have done the Self-Awareness Exercises. How fulfilled are you presently? Circle T if the statement is mostly true for you or F is the statement is mostly false for you.

1. My work/career is energizing to me. It doesn't drain me. (T/F)

2. I am happily married or happily single. (T/F)

3. I am at peace with the people in my life. (T/F)

4. I have close friends that I enjoy and are easy to be around. (T/F)

5. My work is not all of my life, but it is a fulfilling part of my life. (T/F)

6. I am spiritually at peace. (T/F)

7. I have a few best friends and care for them well. (T/F)

8. I have my debt obligations under control. (T/F)

9. I spend my leisure time doing things I totally enjoy. (T/F)

10. I take delight in simple things. (T/F)

11. I look forward to getting up every morning. (T/F)

12. I have enough discretionary money for fun things. (T/F)

13. My boundaries are strong enough that people respect me, my needs, and what I want. (T/F)

14. I don't spend time with anyone who is using me. (T/F)

15. I have no problem asking for what I want. (T/F)

16. There is nothing I am avoiding or have apprehension about. (T/F)

17. I know what my goals are, and I am steadily making progress to make them areality. (T/F)

18. I am energetic throughout the day; I usually don't feel exhausted. (T/F)

19. My personal needs have been satisfied; I am not driven by unmet needs. (T/F)

20. I don't procrastinate to get things done. I feel on top of what I need to get accomplished. (T/F)

21. I know my personal values, and my life is oriented around them. (T/F)

22. My home brings me joy every time I walk inside. (T/F)

23. I am taking good care of my body and receiving proper, effective care for any health problems I have. (T/F)

24. I am living my life, not the life that someone else designed for me or expected of me. (T/F)

25. I reduce stress daily by praying, meditating, taking a long bath, exercising, walking, etc. (T/F)

26. I simply enjoy my life and focus on what fulfills me. (T/F)

27. I choose to only be around people that are good for me. (T/F)

28. There is nothing I am not facing head-on. I am not stuck. (T/F)

29. I have at least an hour a day that is exclusively for me, and I spend it how I choose. (T/F)

30. I don't live with regrets. (T/F)

SCORING KEY

Give yourself one point for every statement that you said is true for you.

27–30 Amazing!
Congrats! Your results say you scored Amazing. That means you are self-aware and live your life intentionally.

22–26 Great Job!
Congrats! Your results say you scored Great Job! Though this is a tough test, your score is very high—but you may have a few areas you would like to improve.

16–21 Pretty Good!
Congrats! Your results say you scored Not So Bad! Okay, you fall in the average zone; that's not so bad, but with a little work, you can experience greater fulfillment.

11–15 Need a Little Help!
Time for some self-reflection to understand why you feel the way you do. Is there any area you can make changes in? Is it a temporary condition, or have you just not paid attention to your life yet? Make it a goal to work on the area that needs improvement. Then retake this test in 2-4-6 weeks to see how you are doing.

0–10 Time for Some Serious Work—Your Life Is Calling!
It's not too late to have an enjoyable and meaningful life, but it won't happen without some old-fashioned hard work. No time to wait and see if your life will turn around on its own. Invest in yourself. Be intentional about change. Find someone to help you—a coach, counselor, pastor, or friend. Make it a goal to work on two areas that need improvement. Then retake this test in 2-4-6 weeks to see how you are doing.

EXERCISE II: THE *AWARE LIFE* FULFILLMENT SCALE

Describe the <u>current</u> condition of your life. For each of the life areas listed below, assign a satisfaction rating using a scale of 1 through 10, with 10 being most satisfied and 1 being least satisfied.

___ Primary Relationship (spouse, partner, most intimate relationship)

___ Family (children and/or extended family)

___ Friends/Community

___ Home Environment

___ Appearance

___ Health

___ Work

___ Finances/Money

___ Personal Growth

___ Spirituality

___ Recreation

- Now focus on what fulfillment would look like for you in each life area, paying particular attention to those where your scores are the lowest. Picture each area—and how it would look—if it was 10. Focus on what you really want and what your life would be like if you were the most satisfied and thriving in every dimension. Write a note to yourself on how each category would look if it were a 10.

EXERCISE III: CHECKLIST FOR PERSONAL VALUES

Below is a list of personal values (both work and personal). Select the ten that are most important to you.

- ☐ Achievement
- ☐ Advancement and promotion
- ☐ Adventure
- ☐ Affection
- ☐ Arts
- ☐ Change
- ☐ Community
- ☐ Competence
- ☐ Competition
- ☐ Cooperation
- ☐ Country
- ☐ Creativity
- ☐ Democracy
- ☐ Economic security
- ☐ Ethical practice
- ☐ Excellence
- ☐ Fame
- ☐ Family
- ☐ Friendships
- ☐ Growth
- ☐ Righteousness

- ☐ Helping others
- ☐ Honesty
- ☐ Independence
- ☐ Influencing Others
- ☐ Inner harmony
- ☐ Integrity
- ☐ Intellectual status
- ☐ Leadership
- ☐ Love
- ☐ Loyalty
- ☐ Meaningful work
- ☐ Money
- ☐ Nature
- ☐ Being around honest people
- ☐ Order (tranquility, stability, conformity)
- ☐ Physical challenge
- ☐ Pleasure
- ☐ Power and authority
- ☐ Privacy
- ☐ Public service
- ☐ Purity
- ☐ Recognition
- ☐ Religion
- ☐ Reputation
- ☐ Responsibility
- ☐ Self-respect

- ☐ Stability
- ☐ Status
- ☐ Spirituality/Faith
- ☐ Working alone
- ☐ Wisdom

1. Which of your top ten values are the top five values you desire in your personal life?

    1. _____
    2. _____
    3. _____
    4. _____
    5. _____

2. Which of your top ten values are the top five values you desire in your work life? (you can duplicate any value you feel falls into both of these categories)

    1. _____
    2. _____
    3. _____
    4. _____
    5. _____

3. Which of your top ten values are not being met in your life today?

    1. _____
    2. _____
    3. _____

4. How can you be more intentional to incorporate the above values in your life?

___
___
___
___

EXERCISE IV: FINDING CORE VALUES

Typically, each of us has three to five core values—values that have been with us for most of our lives. I invite you to discover more about these values. Using the list from Exercise III, answer the questions below:

1. Think back to the values you had as a child. List up to five qualities that were true of you between the ages of five and ten.

   Below are some questions to help you remember your childhood:

   - What did you like to do for fun?

   - Were you a creative child?

- Did you love nature, animals, cooking, sports, building forts, or imaginary play?

- Were you a natural helper of others?

- Which toys did you mostly play with?

- Did you love to experiment, adventure, and explore?

2. After you have made your list of childhood values, then:

    1) Which values do you still notice in your life?

    2) Which ones are you no longer experiencing or honoring?

3) Is there an area of your life that you used to enjoy but are now neglecting? What is it? How can you reintroduce this value back into your life?

4) What relationships in your present life support and enrich your values?

5) Does your career currently align with your values? If not, which value or values are you not honoring?

3. Ask three people who know you well what they think your values are. Sometimes our values are more obvious to others than they are to us. Your values show up in the decisions you make and in the work you choose. In many ways, your values are who you are; your values are key driving forces.

4. Using the answers above, write your core values here:

EXERCISE V: QUESTIONS TO ASK YOURSELF

Insight comes from taking the time to ask yourself questions. Give yourself plenty of time to do this exercise. Contemplate on one or all of the questions below. Use them as your guide to start the process of aligning your life with your true-self. Remember, there is no right or wrong answer, only insight. Write down a phrase or sentence for each question. Note: After reviewing these questions, spend some time in reflection and journal your thoughts.

- How would you describe your life up to this point?

- What is the most important value in your life?

- What are the primary emotions that drive your life?

- What do you do for fun?

- When do you feel most fulfilled?

- When do you feel at peace or most relaxed?

- Do you have any dreams or goals you have let go?

- If you had no restrictions, what would your perfect/ideal day look like (from the time you wake until you fall asleep)?

- What is preventing you from your perfect/ideal day?

EXERCISE VI: INTENTIONAL ACTIONS

One simple change in your life can transform your entire life. By choosing to live intentionally, you can slowly but surely develop the life you always wanted. The *aware life* is an ongoing quality-of-life shift. It is about living fully and with purpose. Creating the life of fulfillment you desire. "I am intentional to experience more joy, connection, and creativity in my work" is an example of the *Aware Life*. Whereas Intentional Actions are behaviors; what action you are going to do to achieve this particular aspect of your *aware life*.

	Aware Life	**Intentional Actions**
Primary Relationship:	1._____	1._____
	2._____	2._____
Family:	1._____	1._____
	2._____	2._____
Friends/Community:	1._____	1._____
	2._____	2._____
Home Environment:	1._____	1._____
	2._____	2._____
Appearance:	1._____	1._____

SELF-AWARENESS EXERCISES

	2.	2.
Health:	1.	1.
	2.	2.
Work:	1.	1.
	2.	2.
Finances/Money:	1.	1.
	2.	2.
Personal Growth:	1.	1.
	2.	2.
Spirituality:	1.	1.
	2.	2.
Recreation:	1.	1.
	2.	2.

EXERCISE VII: PRACTICE FORGIVENESS

A good practice exercise for choosing authentic forgiveness and compassion is the following exercise. Select a person with whom you want to work toward forgiveness—perhaps someone with whom you struggle or someone who has hurt you in the past. Think about that person and repeat each step below.

STEP 1

With attention on the person, repeat to yourself, "Just like me, this person is seeking some happiness for his/her life."

STEP 2

With attention on the person, repeat to yourself, "Just like me, this person is trying to avoid suffering in his/her life."

STEP 3

With attention on the person, repeat to yourself, "Just like me, this person has known sadness, loneliness, and despair."

STEP 4

With attention on the person, repeat to yourself, "Just like me, this person is seeking to fulfill his/her needs."

STEP 5

With attention on the person, repeat to yourself, "Just like me, this person is learning about life."

- What did you experience?

- Did you feel any empathy toward this person—without justifying the behavior of the offender?

- Were you able to let the hurt go—and feel the freedom of not carrying resentment?[1]

*Remember forgiveness does not mean you necessarily reconcile with the offender - it means you free yourself from the burden of carrying the bitterness toward the offender.

EXERCISE VIII: SELF-AWARENESS

Choose Four things from the list below you would like more of in your life. Fill in the sentence.

I Want More _____ *in my Life Right Now!*

vitality	self-esteem	direction
tenderness	composure	security
recognition	generosity	balance
activity	confidence	caring
awareness	health	motivation
sharing	solitude	devotion
contemplation	serenity	trust
insight	joy	commitment
communion	integration	forgiveness
surrender	faith	purpose
music	laughter	support
self-expression	companionship	harmony
romance	intimacy	patience
beauty	sensitivity	self-awareness
skill	opportunity	challenges
variety	structure	accomplishments
control	imagination	money
responsibility	education	experience
freedom	strength	energy
fitness	relaxation	comfort
nutrition	touching	sleep
childlikeness	coordination	flexibility
exercise	self-control	celebration

1. What do you want?_____
   Why?_____

2. What do you want?_____
   Why?_____

3. What do you want?_____
   Why?_____

4. What do you want?_____
   Why?_____

5. What can you do to have more of each of the qualities in your life?

1. _____

2. _____

3. _____

4. _____

EXERCISE IX: YOUR *AWARE LIFE* DEFINED

Now you have completed most of the Self-Awareness Exercises; you have a clearer understanding of who you are and what you want in your life. What does the *aware life* mean to you, and how can you design your life to experience more personal fulfillment?

EXERCISE X: ENERGY DRAINERS

STEP 1

Take some time to identify your personal annoyances and sufferings. Identify any area of your life that is not in balance or is not what you want it to be. (It may help you to look at your lowest scores in EXERCISE II: THE *AWARE LIFE* FULFILLMENT SCALE.)

List them here:

STEP 2

Make a list of what you are losing by continuing to have these annoyances and sufferings in your life. Anything you tolerate has a cost. It may cost you time, money, energy, or even your self-worth. It may cross your boundaries or actually put you in harm's way. There is a price to pay for tolerating others' or your own unrealistic expectations. The cost may include disappointments and will likely impinge on your daily fulfillment and peace. If you want satisfaction and balance in your life, you cannot afford to give up pieces of yourself this way.

STEP 3

Make a plan to change and/or eliminate the list of your personal annoyances and sufferings. You can do this by implementing one of the following:

1. Find a compromise. Look for solutions that will work for you now and will take the emotional drain out of the situation. It cannot be done all at once, but take steps to make the situation more tolerable. Set a realistic expectation for getting some things accomplished.

2. Neutralize your personal annoyances. This can be a more difficult one. It involves releasing those things you don't have total control over and asking for help with things you don't want to do alone. For example, your elderly mother who needs more and more care may be an unchangeable fact in your life. But you may need to call in a caregiver or get the rest of the family to be more involved.

3. Eliminate your personal annoyances. Create a plan for eliminating each personal annoyance completely. You might need to spend a weekend cleaning out your closets and getting ready for a garage sale. You may need to take some time to plan and go on a family vacation, decrease time spent with a negative and energy-draining friend, or delegate work to others at your place of employment. What is your plan to decrease the things in your life that drain your energy? Do you need others to help you? When can you start?

After completing your value work and identifying the areas that drain your energy, you are now on the path of reclaiming yourself and finding true fulfillment. Your journey of awareness doesn't end by going through these exercises. Now you can implement changes in the areas of your life that do not align with your values. Your change may be small or large; it may include adding more to your life or less. What do you need to change?

EXERCISE XI: WELLNESS QUESTIONNAIRE

1. Have I cared for my physical body well by getting enough rest, eating properly, and exercising?

2. How long has it been since I have done something spontaneous and fun, either alone or with someone you enjoy?

3. Have I cultivated the contemplative and quiet side of my life?

4. Have I set limits on my availability?

5. Do I say yes too easily? Do I allow myself to say no?

6. Have I kept confidences, avoided gossip, and spoken highly of the people with whom I live, work, and play?

7. Am I harboring anger or resentment against anyone?

8. Have I invested time and energy into the well-being of the people closest to me in my personal life?

9. Have I allowed myself to fail, recognizing that the only one expecting perfection from me is me?

10. Are there people in my life to whom I can turn in times of need?

EXERCISE XII: FULFILLMENT 30 POSTTEST

Take this after you have completed the previous exercises.

How fulfilled are you now? What has changed? How do you maintain these changes? Circle T if the statement is mostly true for you or F is the statement is mostly false for you.

1. My work/career is energizing to me. It doesn't drain me. (T/F)

2. I am happily married or happily single. (T/F)

3. I am at peace with the people in my life. (T/F)

4. I have close friends that I enjoy and are easy to be around. (T/F)

5. My work is not all of my life, but it is a fulfilling part of my life. (T/F)

6. I am spiritually at peace. (T/F)

7. I have a few best friends and care for them well. (T/F)

8. I have my debt obligations under control. (T/F)

9. I spend my leisure time doing things I totally enjoy. (T/F)

10. I take delight in simple things. (T/F)

11. I look forward to getting up every morning. (T/F)

12. I have enough discretionary money for fun things. (T/F)

13. My boundaries are strong enough that people respect me, my needs, and what I want. (T/F)

14. I don't spend time with anyone who is using me. (T/F)

15. I have no problem asking for what I want. (T/F)

16. There is nothing I am avoiding or have apprehension about. (T/F)

17. I know what my goals are, and I am steadily making progress to make them a reality. (T/F)

18. I am energetic throughout the day; I usually don't feel exhausted. (T/F)

19. My personal needs have been satisfied; I am not driven by unmet needs. (T/F)

20. I don't procrastinate to get things done. I feel on top of what I need to get accomplished. (T/F)

21. I know my personal values, and my life is oriented around them. (T/F)

22. My home brings me joy every time I walk inside. (T/F)

23. I am taking good care of my body and receiving proper, effective care for any health problems I have. (T/F)

24. I am living my life, not the life that someone else designed for me or expected of me. (T/F)

25. I reduce stress daily by praying, meditating, taking a long bath, exercising, walking, etc. (T/F)

26. I simply enjoy my life and focus on what fulfills me. (T/F)

27. I choose to only be around people that are good for me. (T/F)

28. There is nothing I am not facing head-on. I am not stuck. (T/F)

29. I have at least an hour a day that is exclusively for me, and I spend it how I choose. (T/F)

30. I don't live with regrets. (T/F)

SCORING KEY

Give yourself one point for every statement that you said is true for you.

27–30 Amazing!
Congrats! Your results say you scored Amazing. That means you are self-aware and live your life intentionally.

22–26 Great Job!
Congrats! Your results say you scored Great Job! Though this is a tough test your score is very high—but you may have a few areas you would like to improve.

16–21 Pretty Good!
Congrats! Your results say you scored Not So Bad! Okay, you fall in the average zone; that's not so bad, but with a little work, you can experience greater fulfillment.

11–15 Need a Little Help!
Time for some self-reflection to understand why you feel the way you do. Is there any area you can make changes in? Is it a temporary condition, or have you just not paid attention to your life yet? Make it a goal to work on the area that needs improvement. Then retake this test in 2-4-6 weeks to see how you are doing.

0–10 Time for Some Serious Work—Your Life Is Calling!
It's not too late to have an enjoyable and meaningful life, but it won't happen without some old-fashioned hard work. No time to wait and see if your life will turn around on its own. Invest in yourself. Be intentional about change. Find someone to help you—a coach, counselor, pastor, or friend. Make it a goal to work on two areas that need improvement. Then retake this test in 2-4-6 weeks to see how you are doing.

ABOUT THE AUTHOR

Nancy S. Kay

I'm excited to share with you a little about myself and why I wrote this book. As a licensed professional counselor, certified professional coach, registered nurse, author, and speaker, I have the honor of helping people create a fulfilled and purposeful life, both in their personal and professional lives.

After graduating with a bachelor of science degree in nursing from Wichita State University, I worked as a pediatric RN for thirteen years. I then earned a master of arts degree in counseling from Denver Seminary and started a counseling private practice. I am also trained and certified in many assessment tools, including Myers Briggs Type II and Emotional Intelligence 2.0.

I believe that successful living is rooted in self-awareness. Self-knowledge enables people to overcome challenges and live a fulfilled life. In the past, personally and professionally, I have encountered trauma, heartbreak, loss, and grief, which led me to a personal journey of self-awareness. I decided that I wanted to help others learn what I discovered after I recognized the need for BIG changes in my life.

One such change was the decision to use my professional knowledge to focus primarily on being a self-awareness and personal development coach. This refocus of my life has brought much reward and fulfillment.

I am the founder and owner of Grace Counseling Service, Self-Aware101 Coaching, and KnowThyself (KPA) Personality Assessment. Check it out at www.selfaware101.com—it's a fun, personality quiz to help you on your self-awareness journey. Helping people is my passion, and I've been doing it for thirty years.

I have written for numerous magazines and journals, including *Marriage and Family: A Christian Journal and ParentLife*. I'm also the author of *Finding Me Again: A Journey to an Authentic Life*—a journal of my personal journey of self-awareness—which is the cornerstone of *Messy Intentionality: The Imperfect Journey to Self-Awareness*. I have learned how processing my life allowed me to be a more effective individual, author, counselor, and coach. I want to share what I've learned to assist you on your journey.

I enjoy speaking to groups and have been privileged to do so nationally and internationally on topics such as emotional health, relationship dynamics, and personal growth. My communication resonates from my deep passion for seeing people find the freedom and success that comes from aligning their lives with their true selves. One of my favorite quotes is from psychotherapist Carl Jung, "Until you make the unconscious conscious, it will direct your life."

In my leisure time, I enjoy traveling, being in the outdoors, drinking robust coffee, and sipping good wine. But my most favorite time is sharing life with friends and family. I look forward to helping you find what you're looking for.

Connect with Me

Twitter

@SelfAware101

LinkedIn

NancySKay

Websites

www.selfaware101.com

NOTES

CHAPTER 1

1. LaMott, A. (1994). Bird by Bird. New York: Anchor Books.
2. Bradberry, T. and Greaves, J. (2009). Emotional Intelligence 2.0. San Diego, California: TalentSmart.
3. Stein, S. and Book, H. (2011). The EQ Edge: Emotional Intelligence and your Success. Ontario: Jossey-Bass – A Wiley Imprint.
4. LaMott, Anne. (1994) Bird by Bird. New York: Anchor Books.
5. Rinehart, P. (2001). Strong Women, Soft Hearts: A Woman's Guide to Cultivating a Wise Heart and a Passionate Life. Hearts. Nashville: W Publishing Group.
6. Gerlach, P. (2014) "Perspective on Your False Selves: Who's Really Running Your Life?" https://thesevenminds.wordpress.com/2014/05/15/self-in-charge/. (Accessed: September 17, 2015).
7. One doesn't discover new lands without consenting to lose sight, for a very long time, of the shore. Les faux-monnayeurs [The Counterfeiters] (1925).

CHAPTER 2

1. Kierkegaard, S. (1843) Journal JJ: 167, Søren Kierkegaard Research Center, Copenhagen, 1997--, volume 18, p. 306.

2. Hollis, J. (2005). Finding Meaning in the Second Half of Life: How to Finally, Really Grow Up. New York: Penguin Group, Inc.

3. Brown, B. (2012) Daring Greatly: How the Courage to be Vulnerable Transforms the Way we Live, Love, Parent, and Lead. New York, New York: Penguin Random House

4. Ibid.

5. Rinehart, P. (2001). Strong Women, Soft Hearts. Nashville: W Publishing Group.

6. Benner, David G. (2004) The Gift of Being Ourself: The Sacred Call to Self-Discovery. Downers Grove, Illinois. Intervarsity Press.

7. Eldridge, J. C. (1997). The Sacred Romance. Nashville: Thomas Nelson, Inc.

CHAPTER 3

1. Voirst, J. (1986). Necessary Losses. New York: The Free Press.

2. O'Connell, B. (2005). Solution Focused Therapy—Second Edition. London: SAGE.

3. Raitine-D'Antonio, T. (2004). The Velveteen Principles. Deerfield Beach, FL: Health Communications, Inc.

4. Bowlby, J. (1969). Attachment and Loss, Vol. 1 Attachment. New York: Basic Books.

5. Hazan, C. & Shaver, P. (1987). Romantic Love conceptualized as an attachment process. Journal of Personality and Social Psychology, 52(3), 511-524.

6. Sable, Pat (24 August 2007). "What is Adult Attachment?" Springer Science Business Media, LLC 2007. Clinical Soc Work J (2008).

CHAPTER 4

1. Disillusionment. Webster.org. Webster's Revised Unabridged Dictionary. http://en.wiktionary.org/wiki/disillusionmnet (Accessed: June 7, 2009).

2. Goleman, D. (1995). Emotional Intelligence: Why it Can Matter More than IQ. New York: A Bantam Book.

3. Caruso, K. (n.d.) Hopelessness: A Dangerous Suicide Warning Sign (Accessed: October 22, 2008). Suicide.org: Suicide Prevention, Awareness and Support: http://www.suicide.org/ hopelessness-a-dangerous-warning-sign.html.

4. Dreamer, O. M. (1999). The Invitation. New York: HarperCollins.

5. Sabotage. Wikipedia.com. The Free Encyclopedia: http://en.wikipedia.org/wiki/Sabotage (Accessed: June 10, 2009).

6. Emerson, R. W. (n.d.). Ralph Waldo Emerson. QuoteWorld.org. http://www.quoteworld.org/quotes/11630 (Accessed: November 11, 2008).

CHAPTER 5

1. Bloch, E. (1986). Principle of Hope: Volume 1. Cambridge: MIT Press.

2. Cohen, A. (1996). Joy Is My Compass: Taking the Risk to Follow Our Bliss. Carlsbad: Hay House Inc.

3. Seligman, M. E. (1998). Learned Optimism: How to change our life and our mind. New York: Pocket Books.

4. Stress Management. About.com. About.com, The New York Times Company. http://stress.about.com/od/optimismspirituality/a/optimismbenefit. htm (Accessed: December 12, 2009).

5. Dreamer, O. M. (1999). The Invitation. New York: HarperCollins.

CHAPTER 6

1. Collins, J. (2001). Good to Great: Why Some Companies make the Leap and Some Don't. New York: HarperCollins.

2. Charles Caleb Colton. (1994-2007). Quotationpage.com. The Quotation Page. http://www.quotationspage.com/quotes/Charles_Caleb_Colton/ (Accessed: June 19, 2009). 184

3. Baer, G. (2003). Real Love. New York: Gotham Books.

4. Vulnerability. Merriam- Merriam.com. Webster On Line Dictionary: http://www.merriam-webster.com/dictionary/vulnerability(Accessed: March 11, 2010).

5. Rinehart, P. (2001). Strong Women, Soft Hearts: A Woman's Guide to Cultivating a Wise Heart and a Passionate Life. Hearts. Nashville: W Publishing Group.

6. Frost, R. Mending Wall. Writing.upenn.edu. Modern & Contemporary American Poetry. http://writing.upenn.edu/~afilreis/88/frost-mending.html (Accessed: February 28, 2009).

CHAPTER 7

1. Herman, J. (1997). Trauma and Recovery: The Aftermath of Violence—from Domestic Abuse to Political Terror. New York: Basic Books.

2. Gilbert, E. (2006). Eat, Pray, Love. New York: Penguin Group.

3. Self-esteem. Wikipedia.com. Wikipedia: The Free Encyclopedia: http://en.wikipedia.org/wiki/Self_esteem (Accessed: June 20, 2009).

4. Enright, R. D., & North, J. (1998). Exploring Forgiveness. Madison: The University of Wisconsin Press.

5. Smedes, L. B. (1996). The Art of Forgiving: When You Need to Forgive and Don't Know How. New York: Moorings.

6. Herman, J. (1997). Trauma and Recovery: The Aftermath of Violence--from Domestic Abuse to Political Terror. New York: BasicBooks.

7. Rinehart, P. (2001). Strong Women, Soft Hearts: A Woman's Guide to Cultivating a Wise Heart and a Passionate Life. Nashville: W Publishing Group.

8. Dr. Sue Johnson, "Working with Complex Couples: A Gottman Approach for Treating PTSD, Abuse, and Infidelity"(Video Call), Austin, Texas, September 11, 2015.

CHAPTER 8

1. Norville, D. (2007). Thank You Power. Making the Science of Gratitude Work for You. Nashville: Thomas Nelson.

2. Dreamer, O. M. (1999). The Invitation. New York: HarperCollins.

3. Tzu, L. (2009). Lao Tzu wrote "Tao Te Ching" (also "The Book of the Way"). 600 BC-531 BCl. Brainquote.com. http://thinkexist.com/quotation/he_who_knows_that_enough_is_enough_will_always/213341.htm (Accessed: January 10, 2009).

4. Ryan, M. (1999). Attitudes of Gratitude: How to Give and Receive Joy Every Day of Our Life. San Francisco: Conari Press.

5. Interview with Rick Warren. (December 2, 2005).CNN Larry King Live. CNN.com. http://transcripts.cnn.com/TRANSCRIPTS/0512/02/lkl.01.html (Accessed: March 21, 2010).

6. Quotations about Kindness. Quotegarden.com. The Quote Garden. http://www.quotegarden.com/kindness.html (Accessed: March 21, 2010).

7. Ryan, M. (1999). Attitudes of Gratitude: How to Give and Receive Joy Every Day of Our Life. San Francisco: Conari Press.

8. Norville, D. (2007). Thank You Power: Making the Science of Gratitude Work for You. Nashville: Thomas Nelson.

9. Ibid.

CHAPTER 9

1. Brown, B. (2010). The Gifts of Imperfection: Let Go of Who You Think You're Supposed to Be. Center City, Minnesota: Hazelden.

2. Resolve. Dictionary.com. The American Heritage® Stedman's Medical Dictionary. Houghton Mifflin Company. HYPERLINK "http://diction-/"http://diction-ary.reference.com/browse/resolve (Accessed: April 22, 2010).

3. Chopra, M. (2015). Living with Intent: My Somewhat Messy Journey to Purpose, Peace, and Joy. Deepak Chopra (Afterword). New York: Harmony.

4. Dr. Wayne W. Dyer, The Power of Intention: Learning how to Co-Create Your World Your Way

5. ibid

6. ibid

7. Brown, B. (2010). The Gifts of Imperfection: Let Go of Who You Think You're Supposed to Be, Center City, Minnesota: Hazelden.

8. de Mello, A. (1995). The Way to Love: The Last Meditations of Anthony de Mello. New York: Doubleday.

9. Maslow, A.H. (1943). "Psychological Review 50 (4) 370–96 - A theory of human motivation". psychclassics.yorku.ca.

10. Brain Series Part 1 | Charlie Rose, Uploaded Nov 2, 2009. https://www.youtube.com/watch?v=E8zTtOGh3AQ&list=PLA1322DFA3DB62E10 (Accessed: December 17, 2015).

CHAPTER 10

1. Miller, D. (2003). Blue Like Jazz. Nashville: Thomas Nelson, Inc.

2. Hollis, J. (2005). Finding Meaning in the Second Half of Life: How to Finally, Really Grow Up. New York: Penguin Group Inc.

3. Quinn, R. (1996). Deep Change: Discovering the Leader Within. San Fransico: Jossey-Bass.

CHAPTER 11

1. Goleman, D. (1995). Emotional Intelligence: Why it Can Matter More than IQ. New York: A Bantam Book.

2. Ibid.

3. Wellness definition: Health Promotion Home - TWU Health Promotion - Texas Woman's.., http://www.twu.edu/health-promotion/ (Accessed: August 20, 2015).

4. Williams, P., & Davis, D. C. (2002). Therapist as Life Coach: Transforming Our Practice. New York: W.W. Norton & Company, Inc.

SELF-AWARENESS EXERCISES

1. Palmer, H. (1997, September). Resurfacing Audio Workshop. London, England: Star's Edge International.

CPSIA information can be obtained
at www.ICGtesting.com
Printed in the USA
FFOW05n1606131016